Published by
Browne Burton & Associates
Newcastle

Printed by
Athenaeum Press Ltd.
Gateshead, Tyne & Wear NE11 0PZ

ISBN

0 9524207 0 8

George Silvertop

of

Minsteracres

by
Frank Dobson

Sole distributor

Minsteracres Retreat Centre
Consett, Co. Durham DH8 9RT

To
Diana and Emily

Celebrating the
150th anniversary of
St. Elizabeth's, Minsteracres

Contents

Principal Illustrations

Front Cover:

One of Northumbria's best-known artists during George Silvertop's lifetime was Henry Perlee Parker. Born in Devon, he lived and worked in Newcastle (1815 to 1841) becoming popular with a painting entitled *Principal Eccentric Characters of Newcastle.* In 1818 an engraving was made of the painting by George Armstrong and it is this that we reproduce, *by kind permission of the Laing Art Gallery, Tyne & Wear Museums, Newcastle upon Tyne.*

NOTE: Who's who: a key to the painting, published by William Dodd, 5 Bigg Street, Newcastle, in 1861, appears on Page 311

Foreword

THE English Catholic rural gentry of the late eighteenth and nineteenth centuries were by no means as out of touch as might be supposed from their retired situation. For much of the time, of course, they were concerned about preserving the family's landed inheritance, but they were no less intent on recovering both the religious and political emancipation denied to them in the days of Elizabeth I. The campaign for the restoration of these basic freedoms required a patient though determined approach if the deep-rooted anti-Catholic prejudices were to be overcome, that would be difficult enough in any case, but an intemperate or strident manner would be wholly inappropriate.

George Silvertop, the subject of this biography, exemplifies this outlook. Though not so prominent or well known as others in the front-line, he became a confident protagonist of the moderate wing of the Catholic campaign, not only nationally but in the north where some of the fiercest debates on emancipation took place. Moreover, his low-key style cemented a friendship with John Lingard and other liberal Catholics, and it led the government to entrust him with a delicate diplomatic mission to Rome; he was also one of the very few English gentlemen to have been given an interview by Napoleon. Silvertop's role, then, while not conspicuous, was certainly influential, and his biography is well worth retrieving from the obscurity into which, regrettably, it has fallen in Catholic historical circles.

In this study, Frank Dobson has made a valuable contribution to the history of the Church in this country by skilfully interweaving aspects of the ecclesiastical, political and social history of English Catholicism in what was perhaps its most controversial period in the post-Reformation era.

Leo Gooch
Secretary, Catholic Record Society

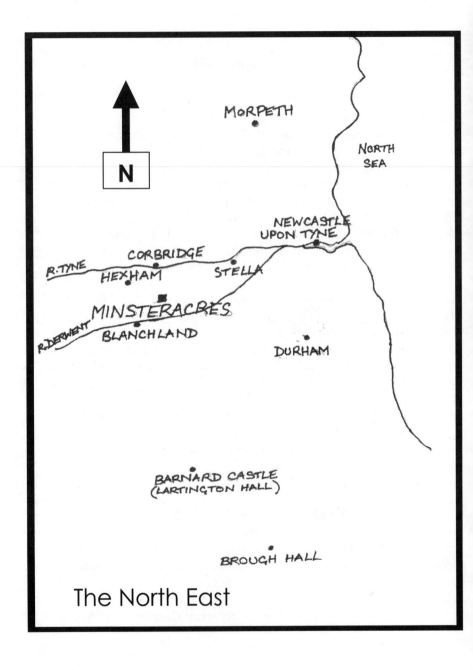

The North East

Chapter One

Turning coal dust into gold

The Silvertops of Minsteracres rose to prominence among the *nouveau riche* of the coal-rich North East in the latter part of the eighteenth century, their considerable fortune founded as much upon the misfortunes of the region's earlier grandee Catholic families, who had dominated the coal industry for almost two centuries, as on their own diligence and commercial enterprise. Sadly, the early Silvertops suffered the same life-expectancy problems as everyone else at that time and as a result the direct male line lasted a mere five generations from the time the name first entered the record books. More significantly, there is no evidence of any additional wealth of consequence being added by subsequent generations, so it is a great testimony to the legacy of the last of the original four Silvertops that relatives, distant and otherwise, were only too happy to take the name (called patronymics, it was a practice not confined to Catholics where substantial estates and fortunes were involved) all the way through the generations to the twentieth century, when both name and fortune were finally dissipated.

Nonetheless, some people are the agents of change while others become its victims. The reactions of all, of course, constitute the materials

1

of history, but their relative importance, objectively, depends on whether they bear fruit in practice (over a period) or wither in inactivity, and in this respect, the writer of history has the advantage of knowing the shape of things that have come to pass. It is from this perspective, therefore, that we consider the true and lasting legacy of the Silvertops: certainly, the fact that the Catholic faith did not disappear in the remote and sparsely populated rural North East of their day was largely due to families such as theirs, together with the Derwentwaters, Swinburnes, Selbys, Widdringtons, Charltons, Thorntons, Claverings and others. There was one among those early Silvertops, however, named George (1774-1849) - the last of the original line - whose life epitomises the family legacy more than most. A man largely unheralded in his day (more to do with his faith, we suspect, than his achievements) he has been posthumously dubbed 'one of the worthiest and most popular representatives of his race'[1] while his laudatory obituary in *The Tablet* pronounced in typically grandiloquent terms: 'He had nothing of that effeminate fastidiousness of the simple and the useful, too common with those of his station, by which they imitate the vices, while they shrink from the corresponding virtues of feudality ... his character made him a welcome guest in the halls of rank and power.'

It also included the thought 'God only knows the nature and extent of his manifold good works, and God, in his goodness, will repay him'[2], words taken from a sermon given on the eve of his funeral by the then chaplain of Minsteracres, the Rev. J. Rogerson, who also said:

> The earliness of the hour, the character of the weather, or the nature of his own engagements never stood as a wall between him and his God.[3]

Now, with the benefit of history and hindsight, we are able to tell a great deal more of George Silvertop's story and endeavour to reveal the true extent of his contribution not only to keeping the Catholic faith alive in the North East, but also in helping to secure for future generations of English Catholics their full integration into the political, civic, ecclesiastical and social life of the country as a whole.

Precious little, unfortunately, survives in his own hand, or anyone else's, to allow us to judge George Silvertop's personal ideals and ambitions, but by piecing together, for the first time, the records that do exist in relation to the various threads of his life – pursuits which he regarded as service in the wider public interest – with his public pronouncements, as recorded by different journals of his day, and those of his letters that have survived, it would seem that he genuinely deserved the approbation, if only for his clear preference for the humility of the cross and odium of being a Catholic rather than the trappings of public office. Given his liberal political and religious beliefs, some might consider him a man before his time, for what we know of his religious beliefs in particular can be seen to have more in common with the deliberations of the twentieth century Second Vatican Council than the rigid dictates of the Catholic Church of his day. As a consequence it is probably necessary to stress that, although it may seem otherwise at times, this book was never intended as a review of the struggle by English Catholics to free themselves from the iniquitous penal laws imposed by Elizabeth 1; it just so happens that this was clearly George Silvertop's over-riding passion and in relating his life's story it is impossible to avoid at least some of the twists and turns along the road to emancipation.

We will begin, however, by paying tribute to his immediate ancestors for their invaluable contribution in providing him with the material means and strong religious convictions with which he was to make his mark. Silvertop, according to the record books, is an old Northumbrian name, although the family were not in origin landowners and little is known of their pedigree beyond the sixteenth century when they appear in the Ryton parish registers as yeomen. Our story begins, therefore, in 1682, when one William Silvertop, of Stella, was drowned in the Tyne along with seventeen others travelling by boat to Newcastle, according to *Archaeologia Aliana*, action had been taken against William and his wife Ann in 1674 as recusants, i.e. Catholics who refused to take the Protestant oath. Records fail to reveal William's occupation but Stella, on the banks of the Tyne, east of Ryton, was the focal point of an important coal-producing area[4] and what we do know is that it was William's son Albert – just fifteen years of age when his father died – who laid the foundations of the family fortune in that trade. It was near Stella that Oliver Cromwell crossed with his army in 1650 on his way to defeat the Scots at Dunbar, but it was the Tempests who were the first family of note to settle in the village. (In 1149 the Stella Estate had been given to the Benedictine Nuns at Newcastle and a community lived there until the dissolution of religious houses). The Tempests, a junior branch of the family who lived at Holmeside, near Lanchester, arrived about 1580 but it was not until 1600 that Nicholas Tempest received the grant of the estate from Queen Elizabeth and was knighted two years later. Ironically, Sir Nicholas' wife became a perpetual thorn in the flesh of the ecclesiastical authorities between 1590 and 1620, because of her persistent recusancy.[5]

It is worth remembering, of course, that during Elizabeth's reign the Catholic Church was proscribed; in other words, it was actually illegal to be a Catholic and many priests and layfolk were put to death for being recusants. The climate of public opinion – certainly towards the death penalty in matters of religious belief – began to change in the period between the arrival of William of Orange and the accession of George 11, but it still remained a long, dark winter for English Catholics. The Act of 1700 'for further preventing the growth of Popery' introduced new measures against Catholics described by Samuel Pepys at the time as 'proceeding to a greater degree of severity against our Roman Catholics than their predecessors have ever done.' [6] As a result, the number of Catholics in the country was reduced to a tiny minority.

The consequence for the North East's coal industry, whose foundation in Elizabeth's reign had been directed almost entirely by a group of Catholic families, was catastrophic; around the turn of the century scarcely any Catholics remained active in the industry. Stella, nonetheless, proved to be an exception. Being the point on the River Tyne from which it was possible to transport the coal all the way down to the sea, Stella had been an active hive of industry since coal mining began in the area in the fifteenth century and predominantly Catholics, because that is whom the Catholic land/coal owners preferred to hire. (In 1767 the House of Lords demanded a census of Papists which revealed that of the total of 793 Catholics living on Tyneside, over half – 457 – were concentrated in and around Stella.)[7]

By the end of the seventeenth century, the Stella estates were in the hands of Sir Thomas Tempest, who died in 1691, to be followed to the grave just seven years later by his son and heir, Sir Francis, who was then only twenty years of age. The baronetcy then passed to his father's cousin Nicholas, but the estates were inherited by his sole surviving sister Jane, who two years later married an old family friend, William, fourth Baron Widdrington, who had been at Jesuit College in Paris with the now deceased Sir Francis. From a devout Catholic family, whose home in the village of Widdrington, on the Northumbrian coast, was ransacked by a French raiding party in 1691, Lord William moved into Stella Hall, and for a while was considered the principal Catholic nobleman in the North. He was also one of the wealthiest Northumbrian Catholics; his wife's Stella and Winlaton estates incorporated coal-bearing lands that were ripe for development. The shallow coal seams in Whickam and Gateshead, to the east, were virtually worked out and, in order to satisfy the increasingly demanding London market, northern coal-owners were about to extend operations.[8]

There followed, however, a traumatic and catastrophic period in Lord Widdrington's life. First his wife died (1714) and then, finding himself drawn into the ill-fated 1715 Jacobite uprising, he was among the first to urge surrender and, with other noblemen involved, was taken to London and imprisoned in the Tower. Tried and convicted of high treason, he was sentenced to death but he appealed for mercy on the grounds that, as he was the last to take up arms, so was he the first to persuade the rebels to lay them down, and in November, 1717, he was granted a pardon. His estates in County Durham, Northumberland and Lincolnshire were seized and sold off and though he was subsequently successful in appealing for the recovery of his Stella estate, the '15 rebellion had left the North in a troubled state, with understandable suspicion and resentment concentrated against the papists, and Lord Widdrington never returned.

The Silvertops, meanwhile, though dedicated to their faith, had taken no part in the rebellion, but found themselves in a battle of a very different sort. Young Albert, now in his middle thirties, with a wife and no less than eight children, had found favour with Widdrington and had been appointed agent, or manager, of the Stella estate. The family lived in a house at the east end of Stella – called Stella House, as opposed to Stella Hall, where Widdrington had lived - and were able to afford to send their sons to Flanders to be educated at the English College at Douay, founded in 1568. Albert had also formed a close business relationship with his brother-in-law, Joseph Dunn, of Blaydon, and between them they leased in their own right several undertakings in the ever-increasing coal trade. This, of course, brought them into direct conflict with neighbouring colliery proprietors – now mainly Protestant as a consequence of the '15 rebellion - who were engaged in forming themselves into a 'Grand Alliance' in an endeavour to take complete control.

The control of coal bearing land, its wayleaves and leases, royalties and rents, turned places into property and property into coalfield. Silvertop and Dunn were clearly too inferior in rank and wealth to be considered for inclusion and letters between Protestant Willam Cotesworth of Gateshead, one of the new owners of the Stella estate and a prime mover of the 'Grand Alliance', and his agent, suggest there were attempts to put 'the two rogues' out of business[9] but it was the inactive Widdrington who provided the vital key that enabled them to weather the ensuing storm.

One of the principal reasons for the internecine battles of that time was the need to secure access to coal south of the Burnopfield line. The outcome was the building of two 'wagon-ways' – the heavily engineered Tanfield Way built by the 'Grand Alliance' and the western waggonway, running down Busty Bank to the Derwent, built by the Axwell Claverings and their associates.[10] Through his wife, Lord Widdrington had inherited a share in the manor of Winlaton, which gave him rights on the western waggonway – and these he passed to Albert Silvertop. There resulted a bitter trial of strength lasting eight years between the two lowly

Catholic agents and their Protestant opponents[11]; in the end it was a matter of give and take but through a combination of dogged resistance and hard-headed professionalism the Silvertop/Dunn partnership had earned themselves a prominent place in the Tyneside coal trade, signalling the rebirth of the Catholic interest in coal. Albert, in particular, had created for himself an enviable estate in the face of considerable opposition, thus laying the foundations of the family fortune.

It was during this period of unrest, in May 1721, that Albert and his brother-in-law decided, for whatever reason, to take a ninety-nine year lease on a small farm high up among the hills and moorlands which overhang the river Derwent as it wends its way down from beyond Blanchland to join the Tyne. The farm, some sixteen miles from Stella, consisted of a small house surrounded by 'a very small portion of land'[12] believed to have been about fifty acres, and was called Minsteracres. It would be at least a generation before any member of the Silvertop family actually came to live on the farm and sadly the history books and records give no clue as to why, how or even when the Silvertop-Dunn partnership ceased in relation to Minsteracres, but the name had nonetheless found its place in Silvertop history.

The transformation of the original farmhouse into the mansion that exists today was to cost the Silvertops dear; later, two separate generations of

Silvertops – John (1750-1801) and Henry Charles (1826-1887) – were crippled financially by the cost. For the meantime, though, Stella remained the family seat. More importantly, the Silvertop fortunes were now definitely in the ascendancy, for if Albert laid the foundations, then it was his eldest son, George 1 (1705-1789), not the subject of this book, who accomplished for the family the giant step from trade to landed gentry. Social acceptance was to follow in due course: George's heir, John, married the daughter of Sir Henry Lawson of Brough, his daughter Mary married Sir Thomas Haggerston, the richest Catholic in the region, and Winifred, his youngest daughter, married John Wright, of the London banking family.

Upon returning home from Douay in 1723 the young George was determined to learn every aspect of his father's business and began as a pitman – a coalface miner - at one of Lord Widdrington's collieries. By the time Albert died in 1738, aged 71, George had both the practical experience and confidence to set about expanding the family business. He bought shares in several other undertakings and made a name for his coals in Europe. Robert Edington, in his *Treaty on the Coal Trade*, written in 1813, speaks of him with high praise and says 'his famous Whitfield coals had the preference of all other collieries on the continent.' George also bought up surrounding farms to enlarge the original estate at Minsteracres although he and his family were still living at Stella House. (He married Bridget Whittingham, from an old Catholic family in Lancashire, who had lost almost two-thirds of what they owned as a result of their recusancy.)[13]

These were still tense times for Catholics generally so George bought a house in London – No. 41 Mortimer Street, Cavendish Square[14] – and whenever trouble threatened he would take his family south until the situation calmed. On one occasion, when the Duke of Cumberland visited Newcastle in February 1746, a mob of angry protesters ransacked the only Catholic chapel. The priest, Father Thomas Gibson, found shelter in a house off Newgate Street owned by George Silvertop in which his mother – Albert's widow – was then living and the house was used as a Mass-house for the next fifty years.[15] The main strength of the Church in the North at this time were the landed gentry and their Catholic retainers; of the ninety-one Mass centres with resident clergy in the early 1740s, seventy-eight were domestic chapels.

The Silvertops (George and Bridget had nine children, including six sons) had by this time established a chapel of their own at Stella House where the priest was Father James Mather-Flint, who was also responsible for tutoring the children up to school age. There were only three Catholic schools of note in the whole of the country and it was on the continent that Catholic England thrived in education, especially at

Douay. The Silvertop boys were sent to Douay, the girls to the Bar convent at York. Meanwhile, despite the difficulties of the day, George Silvertop continued to increase his standing in the coal trade; by 1750 he was one of the lessees of the Stella Grand Lease, alongside giants-of-their-day such as Sir Henry Vane and Sir Walter Blackett[16] and seven years later owned a controlling 62% of the lease, along with many other commercial interests. It was then that he turned his attention to Minsteracres. As a substantial landowner he was entitled to his own coat of arms, which he applied for in 1758[17], the year he began building a new house on the property. The old farmhouse was demolished and the new, single-storey, L-shaped building had rusticated quoins and windows in architraves[18], but it would be another seventeen years before George Silvertop actually took his family to live at Minsteracres.[19]

Long before that, conscious of the religious plight of many of his Catholic tenants and neighbours, who had to travel miles to the nearest chapel to attend Mass, he established the Minsteracres Mission, with the appointment in 1765 of the newly-Douay-ordained Rev. William Gibson, a distant kinsman[20] and nephew of the priest referred to earlier whose chapel had been ransacked in Newcastle. (The Rev. Gibson later became President of Douay College - 1781 to 1790 - and, as Bishop William Gibson, vicar apostolic of the Northern District, from 1790 to 1821 and founder of Ushaw College, Durham). Missions at that time rarely had defined boundaries and the average area of those in Northumberland was over two hundred square miles, therefore it is difficult to be precise about the mission established at Minsteracres, but according to the Rev. Jules Lenders[21], it joined the Hexham Mission to the north west (about eight miles), the Stella Mission to the north east (about eleven miles), the Pontop Hall Mission to the south east (eight miles) and included (to the west) Slaley and (south west) Edmundbyers. The mansion at Minsteracres was still under construction at this time so there is some confusion as to where the young priest newly-arrived from Douay would have lived, but according to the Rev. Lenders, it was probably the former blacksmith's shop at Barley Hill, a quarter of a mile from Minsteracres, where local legend has it there was once a Catholic chapel. Sadly, when the Silvertops left Stella and came to live at Minsteracres - in June, 1775 - only two of their nine children were still living: John, their only remaining son, who was then aged 25, and a married daughter, Winifred[22] - and just two years later George's wife, Bridget, also died. Son and heir John, who was working in the family business, was himself married and living away from home, at Benwell House, near Newcastle, the site of an ancient fortress on Hadrian's Wall. John's marriage to Catherine, daughter of Sir Henry Lawson, of Brough Hall, in Lancashire, was of considerable significance for a number of reasons, as we shall see later, if not for the fact that she was destined in due course to inherit the Maire estates of Lartington and Hutton Henry.

Meanwhile George, approaching eighty years of age and living alone at Minsteracres, caused a minor scandal by deciding to marry again, for not only had the lady of his choice - Jane, daughter of Charles Selby, of Earle – been widowed twice, but was exactly half the age of the groom on all three of her wedding days: sixteen on the first (husband William Ormston being thirty two), thirty at the second (husband Michael Pearson being sixty) and forty at the third (George Silvertop being eighty).[23] There were no children by this second marriage and George died five years later – back at Stella, according to the record books, which suggests that upon his second marriage he had given way at Minsteracres to John and his young family. In any case, upon his death his widow Jane moved to Wooler, where she died some ten years later. And so at the age of thirty-nine John (1750-1801) inherited the Minsteracres estate, together with an income of £8,000 a year. The Newlands and Whittonstall estates alone, comprising arable land, meadows and woodlands, totalled 3,653 acres, while in addition there were six farms in Ryton Woodside (586 acres), Unthank Farm (372 acres), and shares in other lands (e.g. the Broomby Estate).[24] Very little has been recorded about the married life of John and Catherine

Silvertop other than the fact that they had five children – four boys and a girl – but two died in their youth (the second son and the only daughter). The Rev. Lenders wrote: 'John Silvertop continued to work his father's collieries, but he was not so successful. We are afraid he devoted too great a part of his time to the building up of the Minsteracres estate.' The Rev. George Silvertop, in his *Memoirs*, records similar sentiments while Bourn, in his *History of Northumberland*, reveals he left debts of £57,000.

Somewhat unfairly, little attention is given to the part John Silvertop played in the founding of Ushaw College, near Durham – today one of the largest seminaries in the country and celebrated over the years for turning out the best-informed Catholics. Without Ushaw the Catholic Church might well have collapsed in England after Douay College was overwhelmed by the tide of the French Revolution in the closing years of the eighteenth century. Not only did John Silvertop contribute financially to the establishment of Ushaw, and its short-lived predecessor, Crook Hall, but hosted an historic meeting at Minsteracres on August 13, 1798[25], when after years of haggling about the site of the new college, it was agreed to purchase the Ushaw estate for the purpose.

John Silvertop died just two years later, aged fifty two, some seven years before Ushaw actually opened its doors to its first students, but his son and heir, named George after his grandfather, then twenty seven, was quick to take up the mantle and campaigned for years to make Ushaw the premier Catholic college in the country. So, finally, we arrive at George Silvertop II, but before consigning the early Silvertops entirely to history, it is worth noting that, as with most families who rise to public prominence for one reason or another, legends abound. In the North East, mention of the Silvertops is sufficient to prompt a number of off-beat stories, few worth recording, but one in particular has survived the ravages of time in far-off Australia, where there resides, in and around the capital city Canberra, a large family who believe to this day that they are related to the Silvertops of Northumberland, simply because that is what they have been told down the ages.

Their story goes that Mary Silvertop, only daughter of John and younger sister to the main subject of this book, did not in fact die back in 1786 – as all available official records and *memoirs* proclaim – but in fact ran off with a valet called Tom Bell and was, as a result, completely disowned by the Silvertop family. According to the legend, the Silvertop family's embarrassment was compounded by the fact that the young man was a Protestant and they therefore proclaimed her dead. The one piece of material evidence that has apparently been handed down through the generations in Australia to give the legend some credence, is a ring, containing a locket of hair, said to have been given to George (Mary's brother) by Napoleon Bonaparte. (As we shall see, George did, in fact, meet Napoleon, but there is no evidence of any ring changing hands).

Meanwhile, official record books confirm that not only did the ancestors of the Canberra family emigrate to Australia (via South Africa) from Newcastle in the late nineteenth century, but that they had also lived in the West Gate area of the city, in the vicinity of Benwell House, where John Silvertop and his young family resided before moving to Minsteracres. There survives, however, a remarkable collection of letters (145 in all) between the young priest living at Minsteracres at the time and his uncle, in which he refers in two subsequent letters, to Mary Silvertop's long illness, her eventual death aged only 10, and her burial.[26]It seems highly unlikely that the family could have persuaded him to do so in order to hide their embarrassment.

References & Notes:

[1] Richard Welford, *Men of Mark Twixt Tyne and Tweed*, 1888-89, vol. 1, p. 275 (hereafter, Welford).

[2] *The Tablet,* 10 March 1849, reprinted from *Gateshead Observer*, 24 February 1849.

[3] See Appendix (3).

[4] The coal trade dated back to 1248 when Henry III granted to the good men of Newcastle a 'license to dig coals and stones in the common soil of that town.'

[5] William Bourne, *History of the Parish of Ryton*, Carlisle, 1896, p. 23.

[6] *Pepys Diary and Correspondence*, ed. Braybrooke, as quoted by H.Thurston S.J., 'Darkness before the Dawn'*, Catholic Truth Society, 1929.*

[7] W.J.Nicholson, 'Catholic Tyneside, 1600-1800,' *Northern Catholic History*. No. 22, p.10.

[8] Leo Gooch, 'Incarnate Rogues and Vile Jacobites: Silvertop v Cotesworth 1718-1723', *Recusant History*, 18 (1986), p. 277

[9] Shaw E. 'Notes of the Silvertop Family of Minsteracres', *Northern Catholic History*, No.18, p. 9.

[10] M.J.T. Lewis, *Early Wooden Railways*, 1970, pp.119-123.

[11] Leo Gooch, *The Desperate Faction? The Jacobites of North-East England 1688-1745*, The University of Hull Press, 1995, p. 120. Gooch deals with this episode in detail as an example of two lowly Catholic agents of a nobleman prepared to engage in a long public wrangle with influential Protestants, in which the obstinacy of the former is as remarkable as the timidity of the latter.

[12] The Rev. J. Lawrenson, 'Note and Memoirs'*, Catholic Record Society*, vol IV, p. 253.

[13] *Catholic Record Society*, vol. V1, p.179.

[14] Warwickshire County Records Office, CR1291/456/2.

[15] From a talk given by W.J.Nicholson to the Society of Antiquaries of Newcastle Upon Tyne, July 31, 1985; published by North Eastern Catholic History Society (vol. No. 22).

[16] T.Bradley, *The Silvertops of Minsteracres,* 1971, p.16 (hereafter, Bradley)

[17] The Rev. George Silvertop, *Memoirs of the Silvertops of Minsteracres*, 1914, p.10 (hereafter, Silvertop).

[18] N. Pesvner, *The Buildings of England, Northumberland*, Penguin, 1996, p. 390.

[19] Bradley, p.24.

[20] George Silvertop's sister Dorothy married James Gibson, of Stagshaw.

[21] The Rev. J. Lenders, *Minsteracres: The Silvertop Family,* Orphans Press, Rochdale, 1932, p.63 (hereafter, Lenders)

[22] Winefrid, who married John Wright, of Kelvedon Hall, Ongar, Essex, died 1792.

[23] *Gentleman's Magazine*, February 1785.

[24] Northumberland Record Office, MSS Minsteracres. ZCO V.5

[25] David Milburn, *A History of Ushaw College,* 1964, p. 77.

[26] *The Revival of English Catholicism: The Banister/Rutter Correspondence*, ed. Leo Gooch, North West Catholic History Society, 1995, p. 99 (hereafter, Gooch).

Lord Widdrington (1765-1743)

It was he who provided the opportunity for the Silvertops to take the giant step from trade to landed gentry in the eighteenth century

Stella House

The home of the Silvertops
in the late eighteenth century.
It is believed to have been first
occupied by George Silvertop's
great-grandfather Albert, agent
or steward to Lord Widdrington.
The house, demolished in the early
part of the twentieth century,
stood at the east end of the village
overlooking the River Tyne.

Benwell House
nr. Newcastle

George Silvertop's birthplace,
which according to an 1855 directory,
'commanded fine views of the Tyne Valley.'
The house, two miles from the centre
of Newcastle, was used as an
hotel in latter years. It was
demolished in 1970.

Published by kind permission of Newcastle City Library.

The Assembly Rooms, Newcastle

Chapter Two

Three men of Destiny

George Silvertop's life (1774 – 1849) was to span the reigns of no less than four English monarchs – the last of the Hanoverians: Georges III and IV, William IV and, finally, the first eleven of Victoria's sixty-four years on the throne. Much more significantly, though, his was the most important generation in modern history not only of English religion, but of most of the Christian world. It was also the period dominated by two great men of destiny – Arthur Wellesley, Duke of Wellington, third son of a careless, pleasure-loving Irish peer, and Napoleon Bonaparte, second son of a ne'er-do-well Corsican patriot with pretensions to nobility.

For it was just as the young man from Minsteracres was reaching manhood that Europe was turned upside down by the actions of a revolutionary Parisian mob, graced with the title of 'citizens militia', actions which gave rise to some twenty five years of more or less continuous warfare and whose consequences were to echo menacingly throughout most of the nineteenth century. Such circumstances spelled infinite opportunity for those possessing courage, imagination and perseverance. It was a time when *la carriere ouvert aux talents*[1] was there for the taking. Wellington and Napoleon certainly took it – and, as we shall see, George Silvertop could equally be said to have done the same, albeit to a minor degree. Napoleon was to finish up as the virtual master of Europe while Wellington, the man who brought him down, went on to achieve the rare distinction of holding the highest military and political posts in England, a kind of supreme oracle whom everyone consulted for advice. By complete contrast, Silvertop's *modus operandi* was one of quiet diplomacy but though he declined all – bar one -invitations to enter public life, he was not afraid to raise his head above the parapet and speak out boldly in public on the controversial issue of religious freedom, a subject in which be believed passionately through out his lifetime.

With the benefit of well-placed family connections introducing him to royal courts and other eminent social circles both at home and in

Europe, Silvertop earned the respect of all levels of society at an early age, though he was not entirely without his critics. However, driven by an inherent faith, the overriding importance of this particular period in time for him, and thousands like him around the country, was that it was the dawn of an English Catholic revival.

Hopes of the restoration of the Catholic faith - so long attached to the Jacobite cause - had by the late eighteenth century diminished to the point where the highest ambition of the Catholic population was simply to be relieved from the oppression of the Penal Laws. The first steps in this direction came in 1778 and 1791 with the passing of acts of parliament relieving Catholics of certain civil disabilities and permitting substantial ecclesiastical development to take place. Unfortunately these measures fell well short of emancipation and the Gordon Riots of 1780[2] served to remind Catholics that, as papists, their acquisition of full liberty would always be fiercely resisted in certain quarters. By a coincidence as dramatic as it was happy for the members of the old faith, the second Catholic Relief Act – which made it no longer a penal act for a priest to say Mass publicly in England – came into force on Friday 24 June 1791, the actual anniversary of the day on which, two hundred and thirty two years before, the celebration of Mass had been prohibited by Queen Elizabeth. Still faced with a hostile and bigoted attitude from the average Englishman, however, the

Catholic community took time to shake off the cautious attitudes that a background of persecution and proscription had bred, and continued to lead a simple and obscure life. It was the custom for priests – called plain 'Mr' rather than 'Father' so as to avoid detection - to dress in plain clothes; the Roman collar was unknown, and the cassock was never worn except during Mass.

The community in England had since 1688 been governed from Rome as a mission, which was split into four Districts, each presided over by a bishop with the title Vicar Apostolic. The Catholic lay population, meanwhile, was dominated by a small group of families with the proud distinction of being descended in the male line from a medieval ancestor who took his surname from the lands, such as the Stonors of Stonor, the Tichbornes of Tichborne, the Townleys of Townley (who were later to inherit much of Stella) and the Haggerstons of Haggerston. Notable exceptions to this genealogical antiquity were the Welds and Petres, two of the richest and the most prominent of Catholic families in the second half of the eighteenth century. Then there was the Duke of Norfolk, Lords Clifton and Stourton, and Sir Henry Englefield – a select band indeed that young George Silvertop was destined to join upon reaching adulthood, adding his own inimitable contribution to one of the most important chapters in English Catholic history. In doing so, it was perhaps inevitable that the man from Minsteracres would come across Wellington (the non-Catholic who would later play such a signal role in emancipating his fellow countrymen) but the fact that he also managed to come face to face with Napoleon adds more than a touch of poignancy – if not mystery and intrigue - to George Silvertop's life's story.

More of that later, however, for it is important in setting the scene to recall that this was also the time of the twin 'revolutions' of agriculture and industry that between them transformed British society in the most important movement in social history since the Saxon conquest, and ultimately turned it into the most powerful industrial nation in the world. In the North East in particular, the turn of the century – George Silvertop's most formative years - heralded the region's 'golden age' and the birth of modern Newcastle roused extraordinary passions. The town had been the site of a Roman camp, *Pons Aelii*, the monastic settlement of Monkchester, the Norman citadel of New Castle, and the strongest fortified borough of medieval England, whose towering fourteenth century walls were the despair of both the Scots and the outlaw Northumbrian moss-troopers of the Dales. Edward III granted Newcastle the rights of the Staple in the wool trade; Elizabeth signed the Charter that was a testimony to martial strength and wealth in coal, and when wood supplies were low in sixteenth century London, and charcoal failed to meet the needs of a nascent metallurgical industry, the Newcastle coal trade was born.

When Anne came to the throne (1702) there was still a 'County Keeper' for Northumberland, who drew a salary of £500 in return for making good out of this sum all cattle stolen and not restored.[3] Despite the wild moorlands between Redesdale and the Roman Wall, recently so warlike and barbarous, the County Keeper had the best of the bargain as the wealth of the Tyneside mines and the trade of Newcastle began to raise the standard of living for all. The work of making the roads and enclosing and draining the moorland farms of Northumberland, the planting of its beech woods, the building of fine country houses and the making of its spacious, brick-walled gardens, was chiefly the work of the Hanoverian age that followed. Visitors to the region in the eighteenth century often expressed high praise for the more advanced features of the local economy, though there were those who took a more down-to-earth view. John Wesley, for example, visiting Newcastle in 1742, wrote in his diary:

> I was surprised: so much drunkenness, cursing and swearing (even from the mouths of little children) do I never remember to have seen or heard before, in so small a compass of time.[4]

By the turn the century, however, the town had earned the reputation of being 'next to Bristol, the greatest trading town in England' and there was a real sense of excitement and experimentation[5], which came to be epitomised in the works of the architect John Dobson (1787-1865) and builder Richard Grainger (1797-1861). It is said they left the face of Newcastle more dramatically and indeed more attractively laid out then when they found it. Centrepiece of Newcastle's social life for almost 200 years was the building known as the Assembly Rooms, erected by public subscription in 1776 at a cost of £6,000. It was to become a familiar venue for George Silvertop for, as the nineteenth century historian, R.J.Charleton wrote:

> Many brilliant companies have gathered in the spacious rooms and how many happy hours have glided away to the magic sound of the gay dance music since the time when Sir William Loraine and Mrs Bell, and Sir Mathew White Ridley with Miss Allgood, opened the first assembly in the good old time when George the Third was King!

We begin his story, however, back in the spring of 1784, with a letter to the Rev. Robert Bannister from his nephew, the Rev. Henry Rutter, who had arrived a year earlier as resident chaplain at Minsteracres, which he describes as 'a wild, uninhabited place', where he lived 'in the greatest solitude, almost as much retired as any of the ancient hermits.'[6] In an earlier letter to his uncle, Rutter said he was 'heartily glad' at the decision to send young George Silvertop to Douay College, adding:

> I was always indeed partial to a college education, but since I have lived in a family I see the absolute necessity of it, at least of sending children from home as soon as possible. There are still three boys at home, but I should fear very much for them from the fondness of servants did not the father maintain his authority over them.[7]

And so, at the tender age of ten, George Silvertop set off from Minsteracres for a school hundreds of miles away across the Channel, in a foreign country. Accompanying him was his father, John, and on their way, via London (two to three days away by coach) they collected George's cousin Thomas Wright, who was of a similar age. It was a momentous occasion for any young boy for very often he would not return home for the next six or eight years. In addition, up until the Relief Act of 1778 it was as great a breach of the law to send a child abroad as it was to keep a tutor for them at home, while Catholic schools were equally prohibited.[8] Although one of the chief advantages of the 1778 Act was the abolition of the £100 reward for any 'informer' against Catholic priests or schoolmasters, when young George left home it was still possible for an informer to claim the reward against a parent sending his child to school abroad.[9] The journey, therefore, was not only secretive but long and arduous; bumpy roads and jolting vehicles were commonplace in Britain, as on the Continent. For long journeys the travellers would normally hire a post-chaise with postillion[10], especially on main thoroughfares, where a regular change of horses could be obtained at the posting inns. For those travelling to the Continent, the principal difficulty affecting progress was the weather, particularly for those wishing to cross the Channel.

France, Spain and Italy were common destinations for British tourists from the early seventeenth century, but a channel crossing under sail in poorly stabilized ships was perilous, unpredictable and invariably unpleasant. Most Britons had never been to sea before and therefore the shortest crossing, from Dover to Calais on the packet boat that carried the royal mail, became the most popular. There were, of course, other sailings to France – Dover to Boulogne, for example, or Brighton or Southampton to Le Havre, Dieppe or Cherbourg. The *St. James Chronicle* of 20 May, 1769, commenting on the increased popularity of the Dieppe route, observed 'However much this may suit the trading people, Calais will always be the route for our gentry, who had rather go thirty leagues more post by land than cross twenty leagues of water instead of seven.' The three principal difficulties connected with a crossing were adverse winds or a calm, seasickness and problems of disembarkation. Total dependence on the wind led to irritating delays. In 1767, James, second Earl of Fife (1729-1809) complained from Calais: 'Here I have been three days, tired to death, detained with contrary winds, now going aboard at eleven o'clock at night, but likely to be drove back again.'

At times of Anglo-French tension, tourists would take crossings further east. The most common were either Margate or Dover to Ostend, in the then Austrian Netherlands, and Harwich to Helvoetsluys, a packet boat route. The Dutch port was the destination for those who intended to tour the United Provinces and possibly go on to Germany (the Holy Roman Empire) and Italy. A traveller on that route in August 1695, when England and France were at war, sailed under the convoy of two Dutch warships, and had an unpleasant trip: 'Fell to rain and blew hard, which made every passenger sick. In order to land, the passengers were obliged to transfer to a smaller vessel, a fishing boat, always a trying and sometimes hazardous, task.' In May 1699 this same anonymous traveller set out to repeat the journey.

We put four times to sea in the packet boat but the wind being easterly and high, we returned three times back to Harwich and carried out the first time 12 hours, the second time 36 hours and the third time 24 hours, for the most part of these hours we lay at anchor at Owsley Bay and Orfordness and the sea being high made me very sick.[11]

Fortunately for the Silvertops, Calais provided the most direct route to the town of Douay, which stands on the River Scarpe, twenty miles south of Lille, in what was then French Flanders. There is no record as to how the family fared at sea but it was to be the first of many sailings for young George, who became an inveterate traveller in later life.

To English Catholics, the name Douay will always be synonymous with the college founded by Cardinal Allen in 1562, during the reign of Queen Elizabeth, where for more than two centuries the majority of clergy were educated and to which the preservation of the Catholic religion in England was largely due. Cardinal Allen's aim was to gather some of the numerous bodies of English Catholics who, having been forced to leave England, were scattered in different countries on the continent, and to give them facilities for continuing their studies, so that when the time came for the re-establishment of Catholicism, there might be a body of learned clergy ready to return to their country. Little did he realise how long that would be and sadly, before the end of the persecution more than one hundred and sixty of the three hundred priests sent back to England had been martyred, and almost as many banished. During the seventeenth century the memory of these early martyrs was cherished but in the course of the eighteenth century, when the fortunes of the English Catholics were at their lowest point, their memory was kept alive by efforts of just a handful of Collegians, including Bishop Challoner, with his *Memoirs of Missionary Priests.*

The English College at Douay – there were also separate colleges for the Scots, Irish, Benedictines and Franciscans – was of course not only a seminary for the training of the secular clergy; it also educated the laity; in fact, two thirds of students did not proceed to ordination. It was exclusively for boys, beginning at an age generally between twelve and fourteen. The course of studies consisted of two chief divisions – 'Humanities', which lasted five years and reflected the ordinary scholastic education of the period, and 'Divinity', which (in addition to the course in 'Humanities') consisted of a further two years' philosophy and four years' theology. The non-clerical students were known as 'Convictors', those aiming for priesthood 'Divines'. 'Humanities' was divided into classes known as 'Figures' (or 'Rudiments', for those, like young George Silvertop, who arrived at an early age), 'Grammar', 'Syntax', 'Poetry' and 'Rhetoric'. When a boy had finished 'Rhetoric' his school days were generally at an end and he returned to England, but some academically minded lay students stayed on for a further two-year course in philosophy as partial substitute for the university education they were denied at home. 'Divines', meanwhile, would remain at College until their ordination to the priesthood around the age of twenty-five. Clerical students in poor circumstances were supported by funds established in England specially for the purpose, those these did not always cover expenditure on books and other extras and some senior students were obliged to act as tutor to a wealthy, less academic student, in order to make up the shortfall. For those that could afford it, however, like the Silvertops, the annual fee, or pension, was £20 for each student.

Schoolboy letters do not often survive – certainly none from the Silvertops – but a there exists a collection from members of the Trappes family from Yorkshire who attended Douay in the late seventeenth century. Published in 1999 they reveal a little of what it was like to be a schoolboy at Douay – the themes of pocket money, illness, injury, delayed correspondence and the need for various items from home (like fur gloves!!) will be familiar to those who have ever written or received such letters. One, in particular, reveals that Francis Trappe, the eldest of two brothers, was unhappy at Douay - a sentiment doubtless enhanced by the fact that the younger brother enjoyed it – and was returning home after fifteen months. Addressed to his father, it was written in October 1677:

> Deare father, I have wright 2 or 3 lines in hast which will explicate unto you what I have done in business of very great importance some occasions being given to me and other 2 we are about going from the college and doe intend to be with you as shortly as possibly can, and in the meane time I hope you will not be displeased at me for when you will know the reason, which I shall declare unto you more plainly by words then I can by my pen, I am of that opinion that you will be very well satisfied, and if you will be pleased to meet me or to send some others if you cannot with conveniency you will doe me a very great kindness, as for my brother he is in good health and he gives his service to you and all his brothers and sisters and likewise we rest your most dutiful sons. Francis Trappes.

An indication of the possible problem – not unfamiliar in most schools to this day - appears in a letter to the boys' father a month earlier from Father Thomas Lockwood, one of the Douay professors, who in referring to young Francis, wrote: 'Facile and easy natures in a College as ours is, are subject to ye insolence of those who play upon others humours.' [12]

A more illuminating account of life at Douay a century later comes from the pen of the Rev. Robert Bannister (*qv*), who as student and later professor spent a total of twenty eight years at the college (1741–1769). His reminiscences were published in 1979 by *Ushaw Magazine* under the title *Life at Douay after 1750* and included extracts from the correspondence between Bannister and his nephew, Henry Rutter, for 30 years the chaplain at Minsteracres, who was himself also ordained at Douay. Firstly, writing around the turn of the century to the Rev. Thomas Eyre at Ushaw College, Durham, Bannister recalls:

> The discipline and practice and customs of Douay College have been altered and changed since I first knew it ... I lodged in the great dormitory about 7 months, in a small room no one could see me undress or dress me. (Sic) A prefect (whose bed and chamber were at the south end) walked round to see that everyone was in bed, after which he put out the two sconces of lighted chandeliers. In the morning at 6 o'clock he waked us, and all that wore hair (i.e., a wig) were obliged to comb it with two combs, one for lice, the other for putting it in order. This being done all went down to the well to wash their hands and face, and then without

delay go to Church to hear Mass. All the (other) students of every class, whether scholars, Divines (i.e., clerical students), Professors or Masters of Divinity, were waked by a sounding clapper in the hands of the Porter at 5 o'clock, and according to the inviolable rule of the College they were obliged to be in Church at half past five; at the same hour a lesson was read by a Priest, and if a student came not into the Church before it was ended, he lost his breakfast that morning. The fear of losing breakfast made some of them come in to Church sometimes without washing and in awkward dressing. Common Mass (i.e. with the younger students, at 6.30), that is a Mass said every morning by the Hebdomedarium for the Conversion of England and Scotland was never omitted (till the Revolution) at which all the Priests attended. But slothful, lazy, sleepy boys received none or very little profit thereby, and their half hour's meditation before Mass was too often of very little fruit or advantage. This reflection makes me lament for myself and others that were not diligently and more frequently and even every day, by pressing words, aroused to a devout and fervent attention to Mass and its Mysteries, and above all to adore and honour the real and true presence of Jesus Christ in the tabernacle upon the High

Altar. A general prefect is or ought to be a man of great prudence and vigilance in watching and observing the behaviour, the comportment, the negligence, the sloth, the yawning, the lolling of untaught boys.

As regards 'sleeping in', there is a further reference in a later letter when, answering his nephew's questions about a particular boy, Bannister writes:

I perfectly remember his father at Douay College. He came thither about the age of fourteen, after hunting, sporting, without control (for he lost his father at the age of seven or eight or sooner) indulged, caressed etc; hating schools and books and studies. The Prefect went almost every morning to call him up; he lost his breakfast therefore; was compelled to steal it, or send out for it, or get a friend to bring it in from the Refectory, as he had money, as often as he pleased two or three hung on him (for it was necessary to be dexterous to get one). The nicknamed him Justice Breadenell and Broody oftener, to imitate his frowning, huffing, passionate behaviour. He was very fond of handball, but could not endure to be overcome. He had every day 2d portion at dinner, but mumped it up himself, seldom invited anyone to partake.

After this castigation of his behaviour as a youngster, Bannister continued in the letter to give him a much higher character as a man, one of his recommendations being that he 'has kept the same Priest in his house near 40 years.'

Bannister's letters to his nephew begin just a few weeks after Henry Rutter arrived at Douay and he writes:

> I need not send you advice; it is a commodity very cheap, and easy to be found in your own house. Discernment is indeed necessary to distinguish what is good from what is bad, but that is a gem of rare value, and not to be found everywhere. It is, I believe, like poetic fire, a gift from heaven, not acquirable by study, nor to be taught by any scholastic methods. If you could take some lessons very privately of a fencing master, I think it would open your narrow, bending breast, and create your chest into a decent attitude. I would give you six livres for this end, not to make you ridiculous, but to do you good. Thursdays and playdays at the fencing master's house are the only times, and before you go into divinity, not afterwards.

More advice on how to spend his 'playdays' followed in Bannister's next letter:

Is it not a good entertainment to go on playdays in the afternoon a book anisting? (browsing?) Not amongst the modern pamphlets, or comedies or novels; nor amongst metaphysicists, which young heads I think had better defer till maturity of judgment descends upon them; but among old books at Basque's, Simon's etc. where sometimes books of great value lie in dust and may be bought for old paper.

Meanwhile, according to the standards then in vogue, the education at Douay was generally regarded as being a good one. At the end of his course a boy of ordinary abilities had a sound knowledge of Greek and Latin, and generally of French. However, the eminent Catholic lawyer Charles Butler, of whom we will hear much later, wrote:

The classics were well taught, but the main object of them being to form members for the Church, they were not calculated to qualify the scholars either for business, the learned professions, or the higher scenes of life. Writing, arithmetic and geography were little regarded; modern history was scarcely mentioned, and little attention paid to manners. But every care was taken to form the infant mind to religion and virtue: the boys were secluded from the world, everything that could inflame their imagination or passions was kept at a distance ... no classic author was put in their hands, from which every passage describing scenes of love or gallantry, or tending, even in the remotest degree to inspire them, had not been obliterated.[13]

When George Silvertop walked through the portals of Douay College with his father and cousin on 12 June 1784, there to receive them was none other than the president of the college, the Rev. William Gibson, who had spent fifteen years as first chaplain at Minsteracres and had tutored father John as a boy. Silvertop senior would have been well aware that this was a difficult time for the blunt north-countryman – somewhat rough of speech and autocratic in action – who had been in the job for just three years. The college had suffered financial difficulties in the past and his critics feared the same again; they said president Gibson's style of management was extravagant and out of proportion to the means of the college. He was to remain another six years, however, before being appointed Vicar Apostolic to the Northern District with the title of Bishop of *Acanthus*. Young George, however, would not have been aware of president Gibson's difficulties, and by all accounts he entered school life with enthusiasm, but there were serious problems brewing on the not-too-distant horizon that he would have to face before leaving.

References & Notes:

[1] Napoleon's own phrase, literally translated as 'career open to the talents'.

[2] The MP, Lord George Gordon, who was bitterly opposed to Catholic emancipation, incited violent disorder in London in June 1780 resulting in three hundred deaths and widespread damage to property.

[3] G.M.Trevelyan, *Illustrated English Social History,* vol. iii, 1951, p. 10.

[4] Norman McCord, *North East England,* London, 1979, p. 70.

[5] Frank Atkinson, *Life and Tradition in Northumberland and Durham*, London, p.129.

[6] Gooch, p. 69.

[7] Gooch, p. 65.

[8] A boys' boarding school was kept by a Mr Newby at Fernyhalgh, near Preston, and at the same place 'Dame Alice' had a mixed day school. The only Catholic school in the south of England was at Twyford, near Winchester. It had been founded in the reign of James 11.

[9] W.J. Amherst, *History of Catholic Emancipation, 1,* 1886, p. 107.

[10] The man whose job it was to go ahead and make sure a change of horses was available at each stop.

[11] Jeremy Black, *The British Abroad*, Sutton, 1992, pp. 15-16.

[12] John Trappes-Lomax, 'Letters from School: Francis and Michael Trappes at the English College Douay', *Catholic Record Society,* vol. 77, 2000, p.455.

[13] Charles Butler, *Reminiscences, 1822.*

Chapter Three

Onwards into adulthood

Douay has in the past been called 'Catholic England beyond the Seas' and when George Silvertop entered its halls the English College had been settled for more than two centuries. In addition, there was a colony of English recusant families in the town, some of who had been there for generations, making it very much home-from-home. Exactly five years on, however, just as he was completing his education and had opted to stay on for the two years of philosophy, events unravelled in France that were to have a profound affect on his future – and that of the College.

It was in July 1789 that the French Revolution erupted with the storming of the Bastille and the overthrow of Louis XVI, although for the first two years of the Revolution, England and France being nominally at peace, the College seemed reasonably safe and the routine of life continued as normal.   The first serious disturbance in the town itself came in early 1792 and was witnessed by two students from the college, Thomas Penswick (later Bishop) and Thomas Gillow (subsequent missionary rector at North Shields) who were returning from a walk:

Women standing in groups at the doors of houses were wringing their hands, collecting parties and as quickly separating, some with terror, but more with menace painted on their countenance, and all tending in one way or another to the great square. Alarm, not less than curiosity, led the two students in the same direction, and they soon found themselves in the midst or a serious *emente*. Before them was a multitude of upwards of 10,000 men, a promiscuous mob of soldiers and citizens, entirely filling the great square. Not far off was a body of troops waiting the orders of their captain, who was in anxious conversation with one of the civil authorities. The mob seemed to be waiting the issue of their discussion, evidently prepared to resist should orders be given for their dispersion. After a short time the magistrate retired into the court house and the captain withdrew his troops, leaving the town at the mercy of the insurgents. Some officers were indeed seen making ineffectual efforts to withdraw the soldiers, but it was only by persuasion; for a great part of the garrison had joined in the tumult, and none of the authorities, either civil or military, dared to interfere by compulsory measures.

This was the first successful outburst of the spirit of anarchy at Douay for, notwithstanding all attempts by the ruling Jacobin party to seduce its good faith, Douay had still stood by the side of loyalty and order longer than any of the towns of the northern department. This unfortunate beginning of the real troubles was occasioned by two of the orators of the National Assembly who had been sent form Paris to spread the spirit of their faction. Taking advantage of the scarcity arising from the late bad harvests, from which the poor of Douay had grievously suffered, they harangued the people in their accustomed licentious tone, attributing their miseries to the rapacity of the rich, and by their violence they succeeded in inflaming their worst passions. In their fury the excited populace fell on the good and loyal citizens, one of whom, Derbaix, was the printer employed by the College, and had become obnoxious to the orators by the loyal tone of his press; and the other was an extensive baker, whom they charged with starving the people for the gratification of his avarice. They hung them up to the lamppost as victims to the cause of liberty, and then spent the night in dragging their dead bodies in tumultuous procession through the streets. Having thus publicly committed these two murders, the town became implicated, and the influence of the well-disposed was crushed beneath the triumph of popular tyranny. Two months later there was the first attack on the College itself, also described by Gillow:

> It was short time before ten o'clock, and at the moment when the community was leaving the chapel to retire to rest. Their attention was first caught by the mingled sounds of many voices, as of a riotous crowd filling the street before their doors. Then followed tremendous knocks at the door with the butt ends of their muskets, accompanied with menacing demands of immediate admission. Dr. (later Bishop William) Poynter (at the time, prefect of studies) and a large body of the higher students were at the moment passing the door. Perceiving that resistance would be worse than useless, he opened the door, while the students stood in the open passage to see the cause of this visit. Immediately four or five of the soldiers in a state of intoxication entered, and pushed forward through the porch and inner door into the corridor. They called out for the young men to be led out into the streets to go along with them. Dr. Poynter attempted to remonstrate, saying that the students many of them were in bed, and the rest were now retiring, and begged that they would not disturb them. 'Where are your prisons? Open your prisons', they exclaimed. 'We have no prisons,' replied

44

Dr. Poynter, and would have added that the young men were free and happy, but the soldiers grew furious. One drew his sword and the consequences threatened to become serious when, in an instant, Messrs (Thomas) Gillow, (George) Silvertop, (Ralph) Riddell, and one or two more, as if moved by a common influence, rushed forward, and taking each of the soldiers by the arm, cried out 'Vive la nationa!' and so drew them out into the streets. The doors were closed and the crowds moved away to the cry of 'Vive la nation!' Vive la liberte!' The students were carried in a sort of triumphal procession through the streets of Douay, and were out most of the night; and in this manner the College was temporarily saved. [1]

It is not surprising to find the young man from Minsteracres in the company of Gillow and Riddell; they were all from the North East of England and had entered Douay in the same year, although Gillow was some years older than the other two. Before the Reformation, the ancient family of Gillow was remarkable for the number of its members who entered into holy orders; the *Liber Vitre* of Durham Cathedral reveals perhaps the earliest, in an entry, dated about the twelfth century, of Michael Gillow, an abbot. Many bearing the name subsequently held positions of prominence in ecclesiastical matters, among them being a president of Ushaw College, a vice president of the same institution, a dean, a canon of the Chapter of Hexham, and vice-rector of the English College of Rome.[2] The Riddles of Felton, Swinburne Castle and Cheeseburn Grange, were another well-known Catholic family in the north[3]. Ralph was destined to become a famous breeder and trainer of racehorses and, as we shall see later, featured in the turbulent fortunes of George Silvertop's younger brother, Henry.

There were two other 'Divines' in the college that night that were to figure prominently in George Silvertop's life. First there was James Worswick (1771-1843), sixth son of an old Catholic family from Lancaster, who lies buried in St. Mary's Cathedral, Newcastle. He was the cause of a particularly dramatic turn of events involving George Silvertop – but much, much later, so we will mention him only briefly at this point. The other fellow student worth mentioning was John Lingard (1771-1851) who was not originally from the North, but became a life-long friend to Silvertop, despite the age difference. Born in Winchester, Hampshire, the only son of a humble recusant yeoman, originally from Lincoln, Lingard had in 1791 been appointed a minor professor, teaching 'grammar', although only twenty years of age and still a 'Divine.'

George Silvertop and his brother Henry had returned to England soon after the incident in

1792 – sadly there is no record of their flight home, which must have been perilous – but Lingard was still at the College the following year when, after the execution of Louis XV1 and the declaration of war by England, the danger became more acute. The eldest son of Lord Stourton[4] was among the lay students of the College, and it was decided that John Lingard should accompany him to England, together with two other youths by the name of Oliviera.[5] The small party left Douay on 21 February 1793 - two days after the *commissairies* of the district had taken possession of the College. A letter written on the very day of Lingard's departure gives the following account of the events of February 18:

> They arrived soon after and summoned the president[6] and some others into the parlour. There an apostate priest and monk of Marchiennes, as a member of the district, read over a warrant, which authorised them to impose the national seals upon the goods and papers of the College, as also those of the superiors. On leaving the parlour, the guards dispersed themselves in different galleries, some few excepted, who attended the commissionaires in the different places where they laid the seals. The guards in general formed a despicable collection – they were seemingly the scum of the town; the commissionaires were equally

unknown to us. The places on which the seals are to be seen are the president's and procurator's chests and papers, the divine's library, the curiosity room, the street doors of the bake-house, infirmary and church. The sacristy was left untouched; the refectory plate in part was seen, but nothing taken. We are indeed apprehensive that when they come to erase the seals, and entire inventory of our goods will be taken, after which term they will be said to be no more at our disposal ... There is no one amongst us who discovers hope, but I suppose we shall linger on a month or two longer ... We have two or three guards in the house since Monday last, the most ill-looking fellows you ever saw, so that we are obliged to have one or two to sit up to guard them.[7]

In fact it was two years before everyone returned to England, the Scots, Irish, Benedictine and Franciscan Colleges all suffering the same fate. In that time the president and forty of his subjects were imprisoned in the Scots College, removed to the citadel at Doullens, thirty-six miles from Douay, then returned to Douay to be incarcerated in the Irish College for three months before finally being granted their freedom. And that was the end of the Douay Colleges.

George and Henry Silvertop, meanwhile, having reached England, made their way to Bristol, where they met up with their father, who was travelling to Bath to collect another son, John who had been taking the waters in the popular spa town. John junior – three years younger than George and two years older than Henry – was a sickly youth. Nicknamed 'Jacky' by his family so as to avoid confusion with the father, he had followed his older brother to Douay in 1788 but after having to return to England the following year because of his health, the College requested that he not return. The Rev. Rutter, chaplain at Minsteracres, writing to his uncle (Bannister) on 30 November 1792 observed:

> Mr Silvertop's 2 eldest sons are at home. John is somewhat better than he has been so that his parents have hopes that his lungs are not ulcerated as the Bristol doctor imagined. George is about 19 and is seemingly a good tempered young man.[8]

John in fact died just six months later. The younger brother Charles, born 1781 and described by Rutter as 'giddy and thoughtless', was still at school at Tudhoe, but eventually went to Ushaw. All we know of his later life was that he became apprenticed to Alex Adams of Newcastle, Hoastman, i.e. importer-exporter, but left to join the army during the Napoleonic Wars, having a distinguished military career, first as a captain in the 14th Light Dragoons, and then in the Spanish service, where he reached the rank of colonel and earned himself the family nickname 'Don Carlos'. In 1816 he obtained Royal Licence to accept and wear the Supernumerary Cross of the Order of Charles III, which had been bestowed on him by Ferdinand VII for distinguished services at Barossa and Usagre. He was living in Rennes, in Brittany, when he died in 1839.[9]

Another Douay escapee arrived at Minsteracres a few months later – John Bell, a native of Snaith, in Yorkshire. He was in his second year's theology at Douay when the College was seized and after affecting his escape, John Silvertop senior arranged for him to come to Minsteracres to become tutor to Henry and Charles. Then the following year, when other Douay refugees had established themselves at Crook Hall, a rented mansion in a bleak and cheerless spot ten miles from Durham, Mr Bell and the younger Silvertop boys rejoined their fellow students. Bell was ordained priest at Crook Hall in 1794 and was appointed Prefect-General of the College. It is said that the suffering endured by the religious at the hands of the French Revolutionaries touched the hearts of the people of England and when the exiles began to arrive, Protestants vied with Catholics in rendering them help. An untold number of French priests took refuge in the North East of England; a report in the *Newcastle*

Journal on 24 December 24, claimed John Silvertop was providing for twenty ecclesiastics.

George Silvertop was considered to have completed his education and was put to work in the family business, but as was fashionable at the time, he also took a great interest in agriculture and became president of the Tyne-side Agricultural Society under the patronage of the Duke of Northumberland.[10] However, he found little enthusiasm for life in the country, prompting Rutter to observe in one of his letters

> His father endeavours to make the country as agreeable as he can and with this in view he has got him a pack of hounds, which I follow sometimes, but very cautiously.

There is no official record of any hounds at Minsteracres at this time (the Braes of Derwent came much later, after the Silvertops had left); Hamsterly Hall and Milkwell Burn House were probably two of the best-known centres of hunting in the Derwent Valley in the eighteenth century. Four generations of the Surtees family kept hounds at one or other of these places, but it is recorded that Anthony Humble's original Prudhoe pack was formed from hounds obtained 'from Surtees, known as the Laird of the Burn, and from Minsteracres.'[11] Young George clearly took to the sport, for a number of Rutter's letters refer to him being away from home on hunting trips. Hunting with hounds has always been as much a social gathering as a sporting event and it was at this time that George established relationships in the adult world that were to stand him in good stead in the years to follow. This was no doubt due initially to the great respect that all levels of local society had for his grandfather's memory, but there were two, in particular, who not only provided perfect role models for the maturing young Silvertop, but ensured he had the benefit of decisive guidance on the road that lay ahead.

The first was Mrs Silvertop's brother, Henry Lawson. In 1771, at twenty years of age, Henry Lawson assumed the surname of his maternal uncle and benefactor, John Maire of Lartington Hall, near Barnard Castle, and inherited the Maire estates, which included Hardwick Hall, near the sea, in Durham, and land at Cotherstone, Startforth, Bowes and Ronaldkirk However, when his older brother, Sir John, died in 1811 without a male heir, Henry succeeded to the Lawson baronetcy, resumed the family name and resigned the Maire estates to his younger sister, George's mother. Described by a nephew[12] as 'a person of strong character and vigorous constitution' and, somewhat pointedly, *'mens sana in corpore sano'*, she was thereafter referred to as Mrs Silvertop Maire. The family seat was Brough Hall, at Catterick, in Yorkshire, and George made many visits there with his mother to escape the extensive building work going on at

Minsteracres at this time. The Lawson family had an extensive knowledge of books and kept a fine library and between 1792 and 1795 Henry compiled *Genealogical Collections illustrating the History of Roman Catholic Families in England that* was published privately. It was said of Henry that he possessed three specific qualities – a high sense of honour, candour and great self-control[13] – and he was a devoted Catholic. Despite marrying twice, he had no children and clearly looked upon his nephew as the son he never had, leaving him £5,000 in his will.

The other highly respected individual who came in to George Silvertop's life at this time was Henry Howard, of Corby Castle, near Carlisle, in Cumbria, a member of England's premier Catholic family, the Howards of Arundel. Born in 1757, he was educated at the Benedictine College in Douay then at university in Paris. His ambition had always been to be a soldier (a path denied him in England at that time because of his faith) so in 1774 he was sent to the Theresian Academy in Vienna[14], which was said to provide the most comprehensive course of studies of any collegiate institution in Europe, attracting students from all over continental Europe. During his time there, young Howard was said to be the only student from England. Howard distinguished himself in his studies and was received a number of times by the Empress Maria Theresa in her palace. Counts Bethlem Gabor, Ranzoni and Monticucolli were his fellow students and among his most intimate friends. On leaving the academy in 1777 Howard's ambition was still to serve in the English army, but neither his father, his relatives, or the endeavours of Sir Robert Murray Keith, British Ambassador at Vienna, under whose eye he had been for the past three years, could obtain permission from the government in the face of anti-Catholic prejudice. After further study in Strasbourg and Geneva, Howard eventually returned to Corby in 1784 where, according to Gillow,

> It was impossible for a person of Mr Howard's frame of mind to remain a passive observer of the great events then agitating not only England but the European family of nations. His politics led him to join the celebrated society of the 'Friends of the People', in conjunction with the Duke of Norfolk (his kinsman), Earl Grey, Charles James Fox, J.C. Curwen and other uncompromising leaders of the Whig party.[15]

On the relaxation of the penal laws, brought about by the Relief Act of 1791, Howard was finally able to achieve his ambition, obtaining through the Duke of Norfolk a captaincy in the 1st West York Militia, and in May, 1795 he joined his corps at their barracks in Newcastle. Not long after he was to be found at Minsteracres[16] in the company of George Silvertop, Henry Lawson, Bishop William Gibson – and John Lingard, who was ordained that same year by Bishop Gibson at York and subsequently appointed vice-president of Crook Hall, the forerunner to Ushaw College. Each one of these gentlemen was destined to play a part in the great struggle that preceded Catholic emancipation, still over a quarter of a century away, and none more so than Henry Howard, who was tireless in the defence of his faith.

For the moment, however, matters of religion were sidelined as the whole country focussed on the dark clouds gathering over France and even before Napoleon seized power (1799), Rutter reported to his uncle

> A military rage has seized all in these parts and everyone is entering into some Association or other to defend his King and country. Mr Silvertop is raising a troop of horse and his son George another to secure peace and quiet at home in case of foreign invasion.[17]

These volunteer forces were known as 'Fencibles' (or sometimes 'Sensibles', as the men were being paid to wait for the enemy to come to them.)[18] The earliest corps raised in Durham was the Durham Association Regiment, which was organised in 1745 at the instigation of George Bowes, of Streatham and Gibside, the Member of

Parliament for the County, with troop commanders from old county families such as the Lambtons, Ellisons, Carrs, Liddells, Claverings and Vane.[19] There is no official record of any troop raised by members of the Silvertop family but Welford's biographical notes include:

> Threats of invasion from the French, under Napoleon Bonaparte, alarmed all England, and fired the youth of every seaboard county within the realm. Corps of volunteers sprang into existence all over the North of England (Northumberland had seventeen or eighteen of them) and over one of these corps, organised in the county of Durham, and known far and near as the Derwent Rangers, young Mr Silvertop was appointed captain commandant.[20]

Young George's mentor, Henry Howard, had set a fine example, raising a force of 220 men, known as the 'Edenside Rangers'. Most of these volunteer corps were disbanded on the signing of the Napoleonic Concordat in 1801 and the majority of the French clergy returned to their country, but hostilities resumed after only a short respite and in 1803 Howard raised a much larger force, six hundred strong which was called the 'Cumberland Rangers'. As for young George, Welford wrote:

In what was known as the second French war, he occupied the same position at the head of the Bywell Troop of the Volunteer Yeomanry Cavalry ...At the conclusion of peace, in 1814, when the corps had fulfilled its mission, Captain Silvertop received from his officers and men a sword of honour of the vale of a hundred guineas.

Much before that, however, events were to take a dramatic turn at Minsteracres. Writing to his uncle in November 1801, Rutter reported:

Mr Silvertop for some time past has been in declining health; he complains of shortness of breath as if he were asthmatical. The doctor tells him in may be the gout and is trying to produce a regular fit of it. A severe one might perhaps be of great benefit to him and restore him to his previous vigour. I pray God to prolong his life for the sake of his family, for his death would, in my opinion, occasion a great change in it, not much to my satisfaction.[21]

It was not to be. Barely a month later George's father, John, aged fifty-two, collapsed and died while visiting the Queens Head public house in Newcastle, and the new squire – two months away from his twenty-eighth birthday – was soon to discover that inheritance can sometimes be a double-edged sword.

References & Notes:

[1] This account is from rough notes made from Thomas Gillow's description by the Rev. John Gillow, his nephew, and later vice-president of Ushaw College. See Bernard Ward, *History of St. Edmunds College,* London, 1983, p. 71.

[2] Welford, p. 297-301.

[3] *Ibid,* p. 309-311.

[4] Hon. William Joseph Stourton, born 1776, eldest son of Charles Philip, seventeenth Lord Stourton.

[5] Martin Haille & Edwin Bonney, *Life and Letters of John Lingard,* Herbert & Daniel, London, 1911 (hereafter H&B).

[6] President Gibson had been recalled to England in 1790 to be made Bishop and the Rev. John Daniel – Douay's last president – had succeeded him.

[7] H&B.

[8] Gooch, p. 202.

[9] Lenders, p.25. Charles Silvertop published *a geological sketch of the Province of Granada and Murcia in Spain,* London 1836.

[10] *Newcastle Courant, 3* December, 1808.

[11] G.A. Cowen, *The Braes of Derwent Hunt,* Northumberland Press, 1955, p.24.

[12] Silvertop, p. 24.

[13] From his funeral oration in 1811 by the Very Rev. B.Rayment, G.V., see Joseph Gillows, *Bibliographical Dictionary of English Catholics,* London, 1885, p. 167 (hereafter, Gillow).

[14] *Dictionary of National Biography*, ed. Sidney Lee, London, 1891, p. 34.

[15] Gillow, p. 429.

[16] In 1800, George's younger brother Henry married Howard's niece, Eliza Witham, of Cliffe, thus uniting three great Catholic families.

[17] Gooch, p. 281.

[18] S.G.P.Ward, *The Story of the Durham Light Infantry*, Nelson, 1963.

[19] *Ibid.*

[20] Welford, p. 396.

[21] Gooch, p. 324.

Chapter Four

Clearing father's debts

It was said of Augustus, the first Roman Emperor that ' he inherited it (i.e., Rome) brick and left it marble'[1] – and so too George Silvertop, in the case of Minsteracres, though it must have been a considerable shock when he discovered the true state of affairs his father had bequeathed him. There were debts totalling £57,624 - some mortgaged against the whole estate – which would have to be settled before any legacies could be met, such as £6,000 to each of his other two sons and an income for life for his mother. As to how his father came to be in this financial mess we have only family gossip, in the form of a brief comment by his great-great nephew in his *Memoirs:*

> My late brother was of the opinion that John Silvertop was not so successful in working the collieries as his father had been. This is very probably the case, as he seems to have devoted a great part (if not the greater part) of his time to building on and developing the Minsteracres estate.[2]

Architectural fashions had altered in the past half century and the renovations undertaken by John Silvertop included adding two further stories – making thirty six rooms in all – and installing the latest in luxury living - bathrooms and water-closets (i.e., lavatories). The main drawing rooms, ballroom, dining room and library were built in the shape of an S, with the rest of the house fitting neatly into the bend in the main shape. The chapel was located in what was previously a billiards room, there was separate accommodation for the chaplain, the Rev. Rutter, and rooms for the butler and other household servants. The completed Hall was everything any architect of the day could have demanded, but it had been achieved at a cost much higher than John Silvertop could afford on his £8,000-a-year income. Consequently he had been forced to borrow from a wide variety of people, and in the end was unable to pay household bills – and even some servants' wages.

The stark details of his predicament – asset rich but cash poor - were laid out in an Act of Parliament[3] which, as was customary at the time, George was obliged to seek in order to sell off parts of the estate to pay off his father's creditors. The man who drew up the Parliamentary Bill for young Silvertop was introduced to him by his friend from Douay, John Lingard. He was the leading Catholic Charles Butler (1750-1832), a man dedicated to learned pursuits who was descended from the ancient family of the Butlers of Aston-le-Walls, Northamptonshire. The relationship between Butler, Lingard and Silvertop ripened into a close and intimate friendship and correspondence, despite the disparity of years; Butler was almost twice the age of the other two.

Since the Reformation the only avenue in law open to Catholics was to practice as a conveyancer and having had his own business since 1775, by the time Silvertop came to London in need of his services, Butler was considered at the top of his profession as a landed property lawyer. The fact that it was simply because of his faith that he could not be called to the bar was a constant irritant to Butler and he became a prominent activist in the struggle against the penal laws. In 1782, at a general meeting of English Catholics in London, he was appointed secretary of a committee, consisting of five members, all laymen, whose objective was to promote and attend to the affairs of the Catholic body in England. That first committee, however, was mostly ineffectual and was replaced in 1787 by another, consisting this time of ten lay members, with three ecclesiastics being added a year later. Butler was again appointed secretary and in 1788 the committee resolved that he should prepare a bill for the repeal of the laws against Catholics. What happened next was to cause a rift between the Catholic laity and the vicars-apostolic, but more importantly for our story, it was a schism that was never truly breached, resulting in a dramatic crisis for George Silvertop many years ahead.

The rift developed when the Committee, in presenting the draft of Butler's bill to the vicars-apostolic for their approval, decided to include an oath containing a new profession of faith, in which they adopted the extraordinary name of Protesting Catholic Dissenters. The oath was formally condemned by all four bishops but in spite of this Butler wrote an 'Appeal' addressed to the Catholics of England which was signed by five lay members of the Committee and two of the three clergy, who also signed a long letter to the vicars apostolic remonstrating against their censure. These papers form the contents of the first of the three now famous 'blue books', so called as they were stitched up in blue or purple covers. Next, two of the vicars apostolic died and there followed a series of intrigues to have them replaced by men who would favour the Committee's point of view, but when this failed and the replacement bishops declared themselves in unity with the others, instead of submitting to their authority the Committee published a 'protest', again drawn up by Butler, and pressed forward the bill containing the condemned oath.

The Committee, it should be explained, was being driven by a group of men from 'old' Catholic families, such as the Petres, Englefields and Throckmortons, whose attitude to the Catholic Church came to be known as Cisalpine; a term which meaning as it does, 'on this side of the Alps', denotes something different north of the Alpine range to what it does in Italy. In

England Cisalpine Catholics emphasised their moral obligations to the state and were opposed to papal influences except in the matter of Catholic dogma.[4] They believed, for example, that the English Catholic bishops should be elected in England rather than be appointed directly by Rome and that their appointment should be subject to a government veto. Among the English Catholic aristocracy of those days, the Cisalpine spirit was prevalent though by no means universal. The man with the most influence over George Silvertop, his uncle, Sir John Lawson, was unsympathetic, but the most formidable opponent of Cisalpinism among the laity was Thomas Weld, of Lulworth, in Dorset, who was asked to join the Committee on four different occasions and each time refused.

Enter here another product of Douay, the Rev. John Milner, a zealous young priest in Winchester, who was appointed by the two new vicars apostolic as their agent in circumventing the designs of the Committee and it was mainly due to his efforts that parliament discarded the oath and Butler's bill fell by the wayside. Writing much later, Milner was uncompromising in his view of the Committee

> Here probably begins that system of lay interference in the ecclesiastical affairs of English Catholics, which . ...has perpetuated disorder, divisions and

irreligion among too many of them for nearly the last forty years.

After the passing of the Relief Act in 1791 the services of the Committee were no longer required but its members, determined to preserve its principles, established (April 1792) the Cisalpine Club, a literary and dining club with the avowed object being 'to resist any ecclesiastical interference which may militate against the freedom of English Catholics.' Eventually, however, a reconciliation of sorts was affected between the members of the club and the vicars-apostolic by means of what was called at the time 'the mediation' and the club was disbanded in favour of a new 'committee' to be called The Catholic Board (1808) which is the point where George Silvertop joined the struggle. Emancipation, as we shall see, was always going to be about the Irish, a point which Silvertop appears to have grasped from the beginning, for he received a letter from Butler in early 1809 congratulating him on a petition 'signed by yourself and several other of our friends in Ireland' calling for a meeting of Roman Catholics to discuss the issue. Emancipation, as we shall see, was always going to be about the Irish, a point which Silvertop appears to have grasped from the beginning, for he received a letter from Butler in early 1809 congratulating him on a petition 'signed by yourself and several other of our friends in Ireland' calling for a meeting of Roman Catholics to discuss the issue.[5]

First, though, we need to go back a few years, and to Minsteracres, where the new squire was facing the intimidating list of his father's creditors; the 'simple contract debts' numbered no fewer than seventy one and ranged from George and Thomas Gibson (£105 19s) and Archibald Rud (£56 11s 10d), both clothiers, to Christopher Blackett (£31 12s 2d), Rudmand and Hall (£27 10s 1d) and a Mr Gaul (£18 10s), all waiting to be paid for hops supplied. Various masons, joiners and labourers were owed £200 and 'several servants who rested their wages in his hands', £700. A further thirty one debtors, presumably the providers of personal loans, were secured by bonds, with amounts ranging from £200 (a Thomas Ridley) to £5,000 (one George Baker), while the principal mortgagees were Henry Maire[6], his mother's older brother, for the sum of £10,000 and a spinster simply identified as 'Ambler', for the amount of £5,000.

An insight into life at Minsteracres at that time is provided by a separate audit of John Silvertop's annual household expenditure carried out by his auditors:[7]

Household servants	Annual wages	
	£	s
Stephen Wilkin (Butler)	30	0
William Binks (under Butler)	14	14
William Jacques (Groom)	20	0

Marmaduke Smith "	10	10
Thomas Carr (Gamekeeper)	18	4
Mrs Blakey (Housekeeper)	16	16
Ann Walker (Lady's maid)	6	6
Mrs Richardson (Nurse)	6	6
Eleanor Arker (Laundry maid)	7	7
Marge Leighton (Chamber maid)	6	6
Jane Sturdy (Cook)	7	7
Marg (Dairy maid)	5	0
Mary Moody (Kitchen maid)	4	4
Thomas Butliman (Gardener)	31	10
Labourers & weeders	29	8
Total:	£213	18

Household expenses:

Butcher	252	0
Fish	27	5
Corn for bread	83	0
Wine, spirits, ale & beer	309	10
Groceries	130	0
Eggs, poultry & fruit	20	0
Seeds for garden	13	0
Total:	£834	15

Even the contents of John Silvertop's cellar were subject to inventory[8]:

		£	s	d
60 doz. bottles	Red Port	90	0	0
1 doz. "	Claret	1	16	0
24 doz. "	Sherry	39	12	0
30 "	Madiera	6	17	6

35	"	Rum	....	4	7	6
80 doz.	empty bottles		...	6	13	4
	Total:			£149	6s	4d

All of this left the new young squire with some difficult decisions to make. Along with the considerable number of farms, plantations and other lands he had inherited, there were shares in Chopwell and Stella Grand Lease Collieries estimated to be worth £10,500. His first concern, however, was to persuade his uncle, Henry Maire to release the mortgage securing his £10,000 loan in favour of an annual payment for life to his niece, wife of George's younger brother, Henry, who, along with his other brother Charles, also agreed to waive their inheritance (i.e. £6,000 each). With the overall indebtedness thus reduced to £47,000 and, wishing to keep the core of the original Minsteracres estate intact, George designated the two estates furthest away from Minsteracres Hall – Ponteland (in the vicinity of the present day Newcastle Airport) and Winlaton, in the parish of Ryton, to be sold.

The Ponteland estate, which his grandfather had bought twenty five years earlier for £20,000,[9] consisted of a mansion house with cottage and three acres of garden, ten separate farms (names like 'Click-him-in Farm' and 'Small Burn Farm') with a total of 2,000 acres, plus five other separate cottages. The Winlaton holdings consisted of one farm ('The Smeales Farm') with

146 acres, 300 further acres of land and more than two dozen cottages and houses, all of which were placed in the hands of two lawyers from Lincoln's Inn, in London, to be sold. The two estates together were estimated to be worth £49,800, but in the event that the sale did not raise sufficient money to pay the creditors – plus the cost of obtaining the Parliamentary Act and the lawyers' fee for handling the affair - three further properties were set aside for possible sale: land at Greenside, in the parish of Ryton, land at Birkenside, in the parish of Shotley Bridge, and Moorgame Hall. There is no individual record of the conclusion of the sale of these Silvertop properties, although we do know, for example, that the Greenside property survived in family hands until the twentieth century. In any event, once the Minsteracres Parliamentary Act received Royal ascent in 1802, George Silvertop was able to get on with his life, squire of an estate now unfettered by debt which consisted of Minsteracres Hall and Farm (170 acres) plus eight other farms with a total of 2,000 acres producing an income of £1,160, and 100 acres of woodland and plantations, all estimated to be worth £39,000, and which he secured for future generations by the establishment of a trust.

As to his colliery holdings, George – rather like his father – did not have the passion for the industry displayed by earlier ancestors, or even the desire to get involved in the day-to-day management, so he simply boosted his annual income by leasing his entire holdings to George T. Dunn & Sons of Newcastle (¾ share) and Matthias Dunn, tenant of Stella Hall (¼ share). Whether he would have acted otherwise if he had anticipated the rapid expansion of the British coal industry that was to follow – output more than trebled in the next ten years[10]- we shall never know but, while maintaining a keen interest in agricultural matters and the productivity of his own and other tenanted farms, he was now able to devote all his energies, and time, to a cause much dearer to his heart – emancipation.

In the April of the following year (1803) George happened to be in London making the acquaintance of other leading Catholics of the day, such as Sir Henry Englefield and Thomas Stonor[11] (later the third Lord Camoys) when Napoleon's sabre rattling resulted in the resumption of hostilities against France (this time to last eleven years) but before returning north, he was to get first sight of an adversary of a very different kind. Silvertop had been invited by his friend John Lingard to Winchester – Lingard's hometown - to attend a special ceremony in the cathedral marking the elevation of the zealous young priest mentioned above, the Rev. John Milner, to the bishopric. Born and baptised in London (1752) the son of Joseph Miller, a tailor, from Lancashire, who used the older version of the name, the young Milner was educated by the Franciscans at Edgbaston, then Sedgley Park and finally at Douay. He was ordained in 1777 and sent to London, but was not given charge of a regular mission. He resided at Grays Inn, where the clergy-library was kept, and was what was known among the clergy as 'a jobber'.

Two years later, however, the mission of Peter House, Winchester, became vacant and Milner took up his appointment in October 1779, a position he was to hold for almost a quarter of a century. In that time he came to be recognised as by far the strongest character the Catholics possessed in England at the time, yet for years he was denied the office of Bishop due to his want of tact and prudence, the vehemence of his language, and his proneness – in the appropriate language of the day – to 'blister the reputation' of his opponents.[12] When a vacancy did occur in the Midland District in 1803, the Holy See finally recognised his intellectual superiority and unassailable orthodoxy and at the age of fifty-one he was elevated to the bishopric under the watchful gaze of George Silvertop and John Lingard, among many others. As Lingard's biographers put it

> There was always the hope that as a bishop he might temper the defects which had marred his zeal as a priest.[13]

It was to prove a hope too far. Milner was strongly opposed to aristocratic lay influence in Church affairs, although he managed to remain on friendly terms with at least some of the Catholic grandees of the period, such as the Welds and the Jerninghams. Not so Charles Butler; indeed it would hardly be an exaggeration to say that by the time of his death, Milner's feelings towards the London lawyer amounted close to monomania and the two young friends from the North would in due course find themselves also objects of Milner's vitriolic scorn and derision.

For the moment, however, George Silvertop had yet to put his head above the public parapet, but in view of the particular cause he was set to espouse so fervently on the national stage, it is worth recording the comments of an altogether more surprising critic a lot closer to home. In one of his regular epistles to his uncle about this time, the Rev. Rutter, the Minsteracres chaplain, wrote:

> George is come to years of maturity and is considered in the world as a prudent, sensible young man. But, in my estimation, there is something wanting in him, and that is the main thing of all – religion. He is, indeed, of a far more amiable disposition than his father, but he is a man that is less domestic, less inclined to the country. He is a man of fashion and pleasure, I do not mean in the vulgar acceptation of the word, as if he were a drunkard, a whoremaster and a profligate swearer and curser, but one who is of an

Epicurean turn and tainted with the spirit of the world.[14]

Leo Gooch, who edited *The Banister-Rutter Correspondence,* suggests in a footnote that Rutter's criticism stemmed from the fact that George Silvertop was a liberal. However, we would offer the view that his use of the word "Epicurean" *[Oxford English Dict: One who makes pleasure the object of his life]* is harsh criticism indeed of a young man who has barely taken a step along life's rocky path and that perhaps the comments of the Minsteracres chaplain constitute more of an insight into his own character, rather than that of his young master.

References & Notes:

[1] In Suetonius' *Lives of the Ceasars,* 'Divus Augustus' sect. 28.

[2] Silvertop, p.13.

[3] N.R.O.404/289

[4] Mark Bence-Jones, *The Catholic Families,* Constable, 1992, p. 67.

[5] *Letter Books of Charles Butler 1808-09,* British Library, Add. MSS 25127 (44).

[6] As explained in the previous chapter, Henry Lawson assumed the name Maire in 1771 on the death of his uncle and benefactor, John Maire.

[7] N.R.O. MSS ZCO V111 2.5

[8] Ibid.

[9] N.R.O. MSS ZCO 1.9c

[10] John Benson, *British Coalminers in the 19th Century,* Gill & Macmillan, 1980, p.6.

[11] Half a century later Henry Charles, great grandson of Sir Henry Englefield and great nephew of George Silvertop, adopted the name Silvertop and inherited the Minsteracres estate after marrying Elizabeth, great granddaughter of Thomas Stonor.

[12] Martin Haille & Edwin Bonney, *Life and Letters of John Lingard,* Herbert & Daniel, 1911 (hereafter, H&B).

[13] Ibid.

[14] Gooch, p. 324.

London bound

Chapter Five

Getting himself involved

Progress towards the emancipation of English Catholics was, it would seem, only ever about the Irish. Bishop Milner, who acted as agent in London for the Irish bishops, made that perfectly clear when writing in 1807:

> The fate of us English Catholics depends on that of our brethren in Ireland ... Our political weight and importance compared with theirs is small indeed. In a word, they are the stately vessel which catches the breeze and stems the tide; we are the cockboat which is towed in her wake.

Back in July 1800, when the British Parliament passed the Act of Union with Ireland, it had been widely assumed by English Catholics that the granting of emancipation would swiftly follow. It was only an assumption, of course, for the laws of Ireland were then, as now, distinct from those in England, but the reasoning was based on the fact that while the English Catholics were a small body, allowing the Government to treat them with indifference, in Ireland practically the whole nation was Catholic. English Catholics, of course, were still being denied the vote – let alone the right to stand for Parliament - and the political affiliations of the leading families were at this time largely to the Whig Party, not necessarily from any inherent attachment to Whig principles, but because of the party's vaguely liberal sentiments. This was not without its difficulties, for to accommodate their own principles with their fellow Whigs of the Protestant faith in order to ease the passing of measures for Catholic relief, Silvertop and leading laymen like him often found themselves opposed to the Vicars Apostolic, and for this reason earned a largely undeserved reputation for Gallicanism, i.e. advocating a restriction of the prerogatives of the Holy See in favour of the immediate needs of the local Church. As it turned out, King George III had his own ideas. Bishop James Douglas, vicar apostolic of the London District, wrote in his diary on 16 February, 1801:

> The last week has been to us a most awful week. Dr. Moylan (Bishop of Cork) had been informed by Lord Castlereagh (Irish Secretary) that the emancipation of Catholics had been strongly debated in the

> Cabinet Council, and had been carried …
> But alas! His Majesty took it into his head
> to resist this determination of his Ministers
> and of the Privy Council … that the
> emancipation of the Catholics would be a
> violation of his Coronation Oath. How
> unfounded is this scruple!

Prime Minister William Pitt and his Tory government duly resigned as a matter of honour, but Pitt's successor, the reluctant Mr Addington, only lasted three years and Pitt's subsequent return raised the hopes of English Catholics once again. It was some time, however, before it was revealed that Pitt had made a promise to the King not to raise the question of emancipation again in his lifetime. The Irish deputies probably suspected as much for in the meantime they had turned to Whig Opposition leader Henry Fox, who had always been a friend of religious toleration.

Fox's first Petition to parliament on the subject, in 1805, was defeated and when he died the following year, the Catholics lost their most influential advocate in Parliament. Pitt had died eight months earlier and Lord Grenville was the new (Whig) Prime Minister, but he too fell foul of the King over the Catholic question. An attempt by Foreign Secretary Lord Howick[1] in 1807 to introduce a Bill paving the way for Catholics to serve in the armed forces was once again rejected by the King and when Lord Grenville refused to promise not to re-introduce the subject, the King promptly dissolved parliament. The ensuing General Election provides us with an opportunity to return to the squire of Minsteracres, for he was on his way home from another visit to London on May 21 of that year when he learned that Lord Howick (a Whig, unlike his father, who was a staunch Tory) had decided, at the age of forty three, not to seek re-election to the Northumberland seat he had held for twenty one years. Writing from the North Yorkshire market town of Boroughbridge, at that time a regular crossing point of the River Ure on the north-south carriage way, Silvertop said he had learned 'with sentiments of infinite regret, that Your Lordship had thought it prudent not to enter the contest' and he would 'console with my native county that we have lost so able and worthy a representative.' He went on to offer his gratitude for Lord Howick's efforts in preparing the Bill which the King had rejected, commenting that had it been passed, ' it would have animated the loyalty, increased the zeal and warmed the attachments of many millions of His Majesty's subjects.' The letter concluded: 'I hope my Dear Lord, that the cloud of delusion which now hangs over the country will soon pass away and that His Majesty's mind may be soon purified of that poison which secret advisers have instilled into it.'[2]

Six months later Lord Howick's father died and, as Earl Grey, he took his father's seat in the

Lords, where he continued to campaign for emancipation and for changes in the parliamentary system. (Years later George Silvertop would campaign on behalf of his son, the new Lord Howick, when he sought election in his father's old Northumbrian parliamentary constituency).

Meanwhile, it was during the 1807 election campaign that a small incident occurred in Durham that is worth recalling simply in view of what lay ahead. It involved a small boy, born in Spain, who was staying with his mother at a house in Durham opposite an inn, where a boisterous crowd had gathered to hear an election address. The young boy, who was destined to become one of Ushaw College's star students, was attracted by a commotion outside and stood at a window to watch. The house, however, was known to be a Catholic one and when the boy was seen looking out of the window the crowd began to shout anti-Catholic abuse. It was the boy's first – but by no means last – taste of anti-Papal hatred in England. The boy's name was Nicholas Wiseman, later to become England's first Catholic Archbishop in the restored hierarchy.[3]

Back home at Minsteracres, George Silvertop enlisted – as everyone was required to do by law – with, in his case, the Bywell Volunteer Yeoman Cavalry – but he requested, and was granted, a two-year exemption, as those at the forefront of the battle for emancipation at national level were preparing to organise themselves into a more effective force, and Silvertop was determined to play his part. Catholic historian Monsignor (later Bishop) Bernard Ward describes 1808 as a landmark in the history of English Catholics[4]; for the Squire of Minsteracres it was the year he began to assert himself. Attempts in the 1780s by prominent Catholic laymen to organise resistance to the penal laws had resulted in the formation of a committee consisting of three peers, Petre, Stourton and Clifford, four baronets, Sir William Jerningham, Sir Henry Englefield, Sir John Throckmorton and Silvertop's uncle, Sir John Lawson, and two others – John Towneley and Thomas Hornyold. Through his uncle, the new Squire of Minsteracres soon became known to them all and it was not long before he was asked by Throckmorton[5] to help canvass the opinions of Catholics in Durham and Northumberland on the 'propriety and policy' of presenting a petition to Parliament in the coming session.

Replying to Sir John from Minsteracres on 15 February, 1808, Silvertop wrote that 'from the moment I received your letter, I have employed myself in that task; I have either by conversation or letter, collected the opinion of almost every resident proprietor of any note in the two counties.' All, of course, were unanimous in their support for a petition that embraced the whole question of emancipation and particularly the rights of the freeholder 'which every freeholder in the United Kingdom enjoys, except the English

Catholics.' Silvertop went on, however, to ask 'of what avail is the whole & unanimous Catholic opinion if there be no lever to put it into motion, no control point to direct its operation?'[6]

Three months later George Silvertop was back in London to attend a meeting of the Catholic nobility and gentry at the St. Albans Tavern in London. The meeting had been called simply to organise "a faithful account" in the press of forthcoming parliamentary debates on Catholic issues, but ended by going much further. There is no detailed record of the proceedings to reveal how the matter arose, but it seems those present shared Silvertop's sentiments, enthusiastically supporting the establishment of a Catholic Board with the following resolutions:

> 1. That it would be highly advisable and useful to have a sum of money collected for the general benefit and advantage of the Body, to be placed under the control of a certain number of noblemen and gentlemen, who should be requested to apply the same according to their judgment and discretion.
> 2. That a subscription be opened at the banking house of Messrs Wright, Selby and Robinson, in Henrietta Street, Convent Garden, for that purpose.
> 3. That the following noblemen and gentlemen, being subscribers, be requested to form a Board for the application of such

subscription: Earl of Shrewsbury, Earl of Traquair, Earl of Newburgh, Viscount Fauconberg, Lord Stourton, Lord Petre, Lord Arundell, Lord Dormer, Lord Clifford, Hon. Robert Clifford, Sir Henry Englefield, Sir John Throckmorton, Sir Henry Gage and J.E.Arundell, William Cruise, George Silvertop, Peregrine Towneley, Francis Canning, William Sheldon, Charles Butler, William Throckmorton, Edward Jerningham (secretary), Francis Cholmeley and Charles Sheldon.

The subscription was well taken up and when a list was published the following March it included all four vicars apostolic, the presidents of the Catholic colleges of St. Edmunds, Ushaw, Oscott, Stonyhurst, Sedgley Park, sixteen missionary priests, ten peers, ten baronets and members of every Catholic family of note in the land, such as Henry Howard and Henry Lawson. Mons. Ward later observed:

It will be noticed that Milner's name appears among the subscribers to the Board. He tells us that he also advised others to subscribe, though he did so with 'doubts and fears'. From the beginning he was inwardly opposed to the Board, looking upon it as little more than a revival under another name of the old (Catholic)

81

Committee. We find him accusing them of paying the Press 'to publish anonymous defamatory pamphlets, mutilated and altered deeds, and false or misrepresented reports of Parliamentary speeches.[7]

Despite Milner, however, the Catholic Board became the standard bearer of the battle for emancipation and within months George Silvertop had helped to organise a petition, led by Bishop William Gibson, Vicar Apostolic for the Northern District, and signed by about fifty representatives of the chief families of Durham and Northumberland, requesting the Board to draw up a petition for Emancipation to be presented to Parliament. The petition, amounting to four specific resolutions, was duly drawn up, attracting the signatures of all four vicars apostolic, including Milner, together with three hundred priests, eight peers, thirteen baronets and eight thousand laymen, but was sidelined by the extraordinary political events[8] in the autumn of 1809 which led to the fall of the government and the appointment of a new prime minister – Spencer Perceval[9] – with well-known anti-Catholic prejudices.

In the meantime, the squire of Minsteracres found himself embroiled in a misunderstanding over his private attempts to find a solution to the vexed question of a Royal Veto in the appointment of Catholic bishops in Ireland. The issue first arose in 1795 and rumbled on for the next 34 years, the Irish becoming more and more alarmed and angry at the very idea of the English Protestants, who had persecuted them for so long, venturing to ask for some kind of control over their Episcopal hierarchy. When the Irish bishops had first met to discuss the matter – in September 1808 – they declared against any kind of veto altogether and the issue, in fact, remained unresolved at the declaration of Emancipation in 1829.

On arriving at Brough Hall, the home of his uncle Sir Henry Lawson, on 11 December 1809, Silvertop found waiting for him a letter from the pro-Catholic radical Sir Christopher Wyvill that prompted him to send an immediate reply. He wrote:

> My Dear Sir - Finding by your favour, which I received here on my return from the Duke of Leeds's yesterday, that you labour under a mistake with respect to what I stated to you to be the subject of my letter to Lord Fingal, I must beg leave to trouble you with a few lines to rectify that misapprehension.
>
> Knowing it to be the wish of many friends to religious liberty, in Parliament as well as out of it, and having heard from you that it was the opinion of Lord Grey, that great good would be effected to the cause if the unfortunate difficulties now existing with respect to the veto could be

got rid of before the agitation of the Irish Catholic Petition, I ventured in giving Lord Fingal an account of the progress of the cause of religious liberty in this country, to suggest to his Lordship the great benefit which would arise to the question by the Catholic Bishops in Ireland holding a synod & in their coming into any conditional proposition respecting the question of the veto before the discussion of the Catholic Irish Petition in the Imperial Parliament.

The great difficulties attendant in the question of the veto are twofold. First, the unpopularity of the question among the great bulk of the people of Ireland and, secondly, the unpleasant situation in which the friends of the Catholic claims are placed in both Houses of Parliament in consequence of what has been stated. It appeared to me that these two difficulties might be obviated by a conditional proposition & therefore in my anxiety for the welfare of our country, presumed to suggest to Lord Fingal the policy of the Catholic Bishops holding a synod and therein coming to the following conditional proposition viz: To consent to grant the Crown a reasonable negative on the establishment of Bishops chosen by themselves whenever the Parliament of the United Kingdom would come into the

Prayer of the Irish Catholic Petition and would grant their hierarchy and independent establishment.

Thus the people of Ireland would see that their Bishops, so far from selling themselves to Great Britain, as is their unfortunately popular cry in conceding the veto, would be instrumental in bringing about their complete emancipation & thus the friends to the question in Parliament would be completely satisfied, for their only object is that the veto should be conceded whenever the Prayer of the Petition is granted.[10]

Wyvill immediately wrote to Lord Grey, acknowledging that he had been mistaken and adding:

I do most anxiously wish & hope that the mistake I have committed may be productive of no ill consequences; & that it may not I lose no time in acquainting your Lordship with it & I also trouble you with the enclosed copy of Mr Silvertop's letter to me, so far as it relates to this subject.[11]

His efforts on this occasion, however, came to nothing and by the end of January 1810 George Silvertop was back in London for a series of meetings regarded by many as critical in the history of English Catholics for it marked the parting of the ways – at least for a time – between English and Irish Catholics.[12] A general meeting of English Catholics had been called for January 23 to discuss the Catholic Board's petition, but was postponed among unfounded rumours that following secret negotiations between the government and the Board, English Catholics were preparing to force the veto on their Irish brethren. In fact, according to Dr Poynter,

> Earl Grey signified to some of our leading men among the Catholics that to obtain success to the petition, he particularly desired that the Catholics should declare by some instrument that they were ready and prepared to give some pledge which should not be repugnant to the principles of their religion, respecting the loyalty of those who should be appointed to the Prelacy. He therefore proposed a formula by which the English Catholics should express that they were willing to acquiesce in any proposal which should be conformable to the principles of their religion, and the discipline of the Roman Catholic Church and which should seem expedient to assure the loyalty of those who were to be proposed to Episcopal order and duty.[13]

When this was put to Dr. Douglas, London's Vicar Apostolic, the following day he was unable to approve it and a further meeting was arranged with Lord Grey the next day, January 31. With Lord Grey at this meeting were Lord Grenville and a Mr. Windham, while for the Catholic body there were Mr Jerningham, secretary of the Catholic Board, together with three of its members – Charles Butler, Sir John Throckmorton and George Silvertop. At this meeting, according to Ward, it was explained that the English Catholics were 'unwilling that any specific proposal that might affect the common concerns of the English and Irish Catholics should be entered into without the consent of their Irish brethren,' and it was agreed 'that only a general declaration should be made, which should express that the Catholics were ready to do on their part those things which, while they were conformable to their religion, might at the same time give mutual satisfaction and security to Government and the Catholics.'

This then became the basis of the celebrated Fifth Resolution which, together with the other four, was written up in the form of a Petition to be put to parliament, but more immediately to be put before the postponed public meeting which had been fixed for the following day (February 1) at St. Alban's Tavern. There was Bishop Milner to contend with first, however, and he was invited to a special dinner at Doran's Hotel in Dover Street, London, hosted by Lord Stourton and attended by six other laymen, including George Silvertop and Sir John Lawson. The idea was to discuss the five resolutions to be presented the following day, but Milner immediately saw it as a scheme orchestrated by his pet hate, Charles Butler, who was not even present at the dinner, to attack him while he was away from his episcopal brethren.

He later described the dinner as 'a bribe' which he argued 'was for the express purpose of getting me to consent to important matters relative to religion without their [the other bishops] participation.' As to the Fifth Resolution, he 'saw very plainly the veto lurking behind it' and when it came before the public meeting at St. Alban's Tavern the following day, attended by about one hundred Catholics, he pleaded for at least a postponement of the consideration of it, to allow time for him to obtain instructions from the Irish Bishops. The meeting was in no mood for delay, however, voting in favour of the Petition in its entirety and later that evening George Silvertop hosted a dinner at his hotel, the Clarendon, in Bond Street, which even Milner attended, suggesting that even he had not yet realised just how serious contention over the Fifth Resolution would become. Once its signing became known in Ireland, however, 'nothing was heard but that the English Catholics had betrayed their brethren' [14] and on St Patrick's Day, the preacher in the Cathedral at Cork, denounced the English Catholics, with the single exception of Dr. Milner, as a fallen Church.

On two further occasions the question of Emancipation came before the House of Commons – to be defeated – and it would be another three years of heated and frequently bitter debate on both sides of the Irish Sea before The Catholic Relief Bill was passed, in February, 1813, under Lord Liverpool's new government, giving Catholics practically all they asked for. Regrettably, this was not the end of the problem. Before the bill's second reading George Canning, who had refused to join Lord Liverpool's cabinet, said he 'cordially agreed' with the bill but thought that Catholics ought to pay for their emancipation and introduced two new clauses consisting of provisions for 'securities', including the veto, but in a new form which, it was hoped, would overcome previous objections. The bill duly passed its second reading but for Bishop Milner the new inserted clauses were like a red rag to a bull.

He immediately published a leaflet entitled *A Brief Memorial on the Catholic Bill*[15]in which he argued that the new clauses, if enacted, would prevent Bishops from exercising their episcopal duties. The Catholic Board responded two days later (Monday, 24 May) with a fly-leaf allegedly written by Charles Butler which professed to answer Milner's arguments but concluded with the following words: 'It is hoped that the legislature will proceed in its progress of benevolent concession, regardless of interference of unaccredited individuals.'

This blatant insult to the Bishop did little but raise the level of acrimony which proved pointless, though none could have anticipated what was to follow the same afternoon: During the committee stage of the bill the Speaker, Mr Charles Abbott (later Lord Colchester), a strong anti-Catholic, declared that while the Bill had been introduced to bring an end to strife, he believed it would produce more strife than ever. He therefore proposed that the clause giving Catholics the right to sit and vote in Parliament should be struck out. A long debate followed but at one o'clock in the morning the motion was finally put to the vote and scraped through with a majority of just four. When the excitement had died down the government spokesman rose and declared that the bill without the clause was neither worthy of the acceptance of the Catholics nor of the support of their friends in Parliament and accordingly moved 'That the Chairman do now leave the Chair' which was, of course, equivalent to saying that the bill had been abandoned.

From that moment the Catholic question began to lose ground once again and members of the Catholic Board and their sympathisers, made no secret of attributing the bill's collapse to Milner and in their anger sought to expel him from their number. The difficulty was that they had no way of doing this as the Board consisted of all those who had subscribed an amount of money to the Catholic cause. They had, however, recently appointed a Select Committee to conduct the affairs of the Board more conveniently and to which Milner had requested his own appointment. On 29 May, therefore, sixty-five members of the Board attended a special meeting at the Earl of Shrewsbury's[16] house in Stanhope Street, London, at which two resolutions were proposed. The first was a vote of thanks to Charles Butler for all his efforts in support of the Catholic cause; the second was the 'highly expedient' dismissal of Dr Milner from the Select Committee. The first of these motions was carried unanimously; the second by a large majority.

Writing later, Dr. Milner said that when the meeting began 'a celebrated orator opened the charge with a studied harangue ...' It was widely reported at the time that the person who proposed the motion to expel Dr. Milner from the Catholic Board was George Silvertop, and that Charles Butler had seconded it. Both would years later publicly deny that they were involved[17], but there is no doubt that the 'celebrated orator' on that occasion, referred to by Dr. Milner, was in fact the Squire of Minsteracres.[18]

References & Notes:

[1] Born Charles Grey at Fallodon March 13, 1764, the son of one of Britain's most important military commanders, General Sir Charles Grey, who became Lord Grey. Thus his son became Lord Howick and succeeded to the title Earl Grey when his father died in 1807.

[2] Durham University Library Archives, GRE/B42/12/65.

[3] Brian Fothergill, *Nicholas Wiseman,* Faber & Faber, London ,1963, p.21.

[4] Bernard Ward, *The Eve of Catholic Emancipation,* vol. 1, p.99 (hereafter, Ward –Eve*).*

[5] Sir John Throckmorton, a proud sheep farmer, wagered 1,000 guineas (£20,000 today) in June 1811, that, by sunset of the longest day, he would wear a coat made from wool which until that sunrise had been on his sheep. The wager was accepted by a Mr Coxeter, the miller at Greenham Mills near Newbury, and a crowd of 5,000 is said to have witnessed the event. Sir John won the bet and wore the coat that evening at a celebration dinner at the Pelican Inn, Speenhamland. The Throckmorton Coat was displayed at the Great Exhibition in 1851 and is today at the Throckmortons' Warwickshire residence, Coughton Court, near Alcester.

[6] Warwickshire County Records Office, CR998/GB/12/38.

[7] Ward-Eve, vol. 1, p. 103.

[8] A bitter argument in Parliament between Foreign Minister George Canning and Secretary of War Lord Castlereagh over troops for the Duke of Wellington, who was fighting in Portugal, actually ended in a duel on September 21, 1809. The two men missed with their first shots but eventually Castlereagh wounded Canning in the thigh.

[9] Two years later he was assassinated in the lobby of the House of Commons.

[10] Durham University Library, GRE/B60/9/14 & 15.

[11] *Ibid.*

[12] Ward – Eve, vol. 1, p.114.

[13] *Apologetical Epistle,* published by Dr Poynter March 15, 1812, in answer to accusations by Dr. Milner.

[14] Bishop Milner, *Supplementary Memoirs,* p.167.

[15] *Ibid.*

[16] John Talbot, sixteenth Earl of Shrewsbury and Waterford, was generally regarded as a leading figure among the Catholic community.

[17] *Catholic Miscellany*, January 1827, p. 136.

[18] Ward – Eve, vol. 2 p.51.

Chapter Six

Catholic Biblemongers

The Squire of Minsteracres, approaching forty years of age, was now well to the forefront of English lay Catholics in the North of England and had come to notice a year earlier in relation to something of a national phenomenom among English Catholics about this time which would ultimately earn him a severe dose of Dr. Milner's intemperate criticism. It was in June 1812 that Bishop Smith, coadjutor in the Northern District, was writing to Bishop Poynter in London about a curious thing which he had recently noticed in his own Vicariate:

> Your Lordship must have remarked lately in the newspapers the numerous meetings of different parts of the kingdom for the establishment of Bible Societies. What is the meaning of it? There certainly must be something more than meets the eye. I was not a little surprised to see that at a meeting lately at Hexham, of which Mr Silvertop was chairman, it was resolved that another meeting should be held for the purpose of considering the propriety of forming one of these establishments in that neighbourhood. As I conceive that this distribution of Bibles is found upon the

avowed principle that each one is to form his Creed from the Scriptures independently of tradition and the authority of the Church. Surely Catholics ought to have nothing to do with it, especially as these Bibles have been corrupted and mutilated by the omission of whole books.[1]

A whole chapter is devoted to this so-called phenomenon in Ward's *The Eve of Catholic Emancipation,* in which he describes the circumstances surrounding the birth of The Roman Catholic Bible Society, in essence a Scripture Committee set up by the Catholic Board on 8 March 1813.   Recalling the letter of Pope Pius V1 to the Archbishop of Florence in 1778, in which he gave his formal approval to the circulation of the Scriptures in the vernacular, Ward points out that during the previous sixty years English Catholics had done much to disprove the Protestant claim that circulation of the Scriptures was not in accordance with Catholic practice: e.g., the Douay Bible of 1749 and further editions in 1750 and 1752. The danger of the Bible Society, according to Ward, lay not so much in what they did but in the spirit in which they did it, adding:

When a danger of this character exists, there are two ways of dealing with it. One is to oppose the whole scheme and to

94

endeavour to stifle and suppress it; the other is to try and control it.' As was to be expected, Bishop Milner took the former view, privately railing against the impossibility of 'surrendering his crosier into the hands of a knot of lawyers and fox-hunters.'[2]

Meanwhile, in a pastoral letter to be read in the Midland District, he sharply warned against 'the prevailing Biblio-mania' and 'the promiscuous reading of the Bible.' According to Milner, the Bible should remain firmly in the context of tradition mediated by good preaching:

> Who could have imagined that Catholics, grounded upon quite opposite principles should nevertheless show a disposition to follow the example of Protestants ... contributing their money for putting the mysterious letter of God's Word into the hands of the illiterate poor, instead of educating clergymen, even in the distressing scarcity of clergy, to expound the sense of that word to them.[3]

In a recent analysis of these events the Rev. Peter Phillips surmises that Ward was probably correct in suggesting that the intention of Silvertop and his like-minded associates on the Scripture Committee was merely to show the 'liberality' of their sentiments and practice.[4] After all, there had been a movement among their fellow Christians from the first years of the century to encourage Bible reading by the distribution of cheap Bibles, and it seemed appropriate to show that the Catholics were not as hostile as was often thought to Bible-based Christianity. The Vicars Apostolic, however, were a little more uncertain. Bishop Poynter, who had been appointed Vicar General of the London District upon the death of Bishop Douglas, took the opposite view to Milner, being cautiously supportive and in attempting to steer the Catholic Bible Society on to a safe course, became its president and played an important part in guiding an edition of the New Testament through the press. Butler had at first suggested that the edition be printed without notes but he was prepared to compromise and eventually the Board published a version of Challoner's first edition of 1749 with only a slight abridgement of the notes.[5] Perhaps not entirely by coincidence the summer of 1813 heralded the birth of Catholic journalism with the appearance of a new publication called the *Orthodox Journal* that carried in its first edition a judicious and thoughtful letter from George Haydock, missioner at Ugthorpe, in Yorkshire, welcoming the Bible Society. The proprietor of the journal was a rather fiery Catholic layman from Norwich called William Eusebius Andrews, who happened to be a fanatical supporter of Bishop Milner and the *Orthodox Journal* inevitably became a stage for some of Milner's most intemperate attacks on the Catholic Board and the Bible Society, not to mention his private vendettas against Charles Butler and Silvertop's other good friend John Lingard.

Lingard had by now declined the presidency of Ushaw College (1809) in favour of writing and had taken a living as resident priest in the tiny (pop. 400) village of Hornby, eight miles from Lancaster. His first published work, *Antiquities of the Anglo-Saxon Church* (1806) had attracted immediate and persistent condemnation from Milner, himself a published historian.[6] Writing to a friend a year later, Lingard wrote:

> As to Bishop Milner, he is not satisfied. He grows worse and worse. He says the book is calculated to do as much harm as good, etc., etc., etc.[7]

Prior to leaving Ushaw College Lingard had also published an *Introduction to Talbot's Protestant Apology for the Catholic Church* (Dublin, 1809) and a *Defence of Ward's Errata* (Dublin, 1810) but he was now hard at work, with considerable encouragement from George Silvertop, as we shall see, on the book that was to really establish his reputation, *A History of England, from the First Invasion by the Romans to the Accession of William and Mary in 1688.* The work would eventually take eleven years to complete but at this point, with the Napoleonic Wars coming to a head,

Lingard was eagerly looking forward to visiting Rome where he hoped to gain access to the Vatican archives as an important part of his research. Three other central figures in our story were also making plans to go abroad: Bishop Poynter, to negotiate the return of property, such as the college at Douay, which had been seized during the French Revolution; Bishop Milner, to Rome – the first English vicar apostolic ever to visit the Vatican – on a mission of a much more personal nature; and finally, George Silvertop.

It had long been a tradition among the English Catholics at Douay that upon leaving the college for the last time they would undertake what became known as the Grand Tour, or simply, an extensive journey around the capitals of Europe. Owing to the circumstances under which he left Douay, however, Silvertop had been denied the experience. Now twenty odd years later he intended to make up for it, only much more serious considerations were to turn it into a mission – or two? - rather than a vacation. For English Catholics at least, it was at this point a case of all roads leading to Rome.

In the event, once peace was restored in Europe, it was Milner and Poynter who were the first to leave England: on the same day, in fact - they met at Dover but did not travel together[8] - barely a month after Napoleon's abdication (April 4, 1814) and with the Pope on his way back to Rome. Poynter had limited success in the French capital, though he did manage to put his case to

Foreign Secretary Lord Castlereagh, who was in Paris en route to the Congress of Vienna, which effected the settlement of Europe after the Napoleonic Wars. First though (30 May) came the Treaty of Paris, allowing for the appointment of three British Commissioners to formulate specific claims for the return of appropriated property. Believing (mistakenly as it transpired) that the religious colleges would be included, Poynter returned home on June 5 – but it was not for long, thanks to his arch opponent.

Milner's visit to Rome – it is said he was so anxious to get there that he took only two saddlebags so that he could do the whole trip on horseback - was to be somewhat more controversial, though his original intention had been merely to secure the withdrawal of what had become known as the Quarantotti Rescript. During Pope Pius VII's captivity at Fontainebleau (1809-1814) all the cardinals had been expelled from Rome and, with Napoleon's permission, the business of the Church was entrusted to the aged Monsignor Quarantotti, vice-president of Propaganda. It was to Quarantotti, therefore, that Poynter had the previous year referred the Catholic bill, with its clause relating to the veto, and had received a reply – or 'Rescript' – urging tolerance and acceptance of the British Government's goodwill.

Unfortunately feelings between the 'vetoists' and 'non-vetoists' ran too high for the pacifying message of the Rescript to produce its desired effect; if it filled the veto party with content, it so irritated their opponents that the attacks of Bishop Milner and his allies redoubled in violence. Although he had expressly described himself in the preamble as 'invested with full pontifical powers' and 'placed over the concerns of the sacred missions', Monsignor Quarantotti was declared by Milner and his non-veto cohorts to have 'only the ordinary powers of the congregation', and that 'his Rescript was irregular and of no authority from the beginning.'[9] Ward denotes two chapters to Milner's appeal to events that arose as a consequence of his visit to Rome, commenting:

> If Milner had limited his mission to obtaining a withdrawal of the Quarantotti Rescript, and securing a thorough examination of the whole question with which it dealt, he would have earned the gratitude of all good Catholics.

With his usual bluff persistence Milner secured a papal audience just two days after the Holy Father had returned to the Vatican and he wasted little time in airing some of his more personal grievances. When the Pope began their meeting by asking about affairs in England and whether the bill for Catholic emancipation had been passed, Milner took that as an invitation to open his attack. He replied:

There is no question, Holy Father, about an Oath or Act of Parliament; Emancipation will take place, but not till there is a great change in His Majesty's counsels. In the meantime, schismatical measures have been carried on among our Catholics, as I am prepared to prove to your Cardinals.[10]

Ward describes this as 'a very serious accusation to make under such circumstances, and its very abruptness made it hardly likely to create a very favourable impression.'[11] The Pope is said to have referred to Milner thereafter as 'a firebrand'[12] and while Quarantotti refused to discuss the Rescript with him, Milner apparently found favour with the Prefect of Propaganda, Cardinal Litta, a member of a noble Milanese family. He prepared for Cardinal Litta a written account of his case together with a memorial of his complaints against his brother bishops and Catholic laymen such as Butler, Lingard and Silvertop. These representations produced the required effect for, by the end of the first month of Milner's visit, Litta had sent a letter to Poynter saying that the Pope had decided to refer the whole issue to a special congregation for consideration. This, as far as Milner was concerned, revoked Quarantotti's Rescript, which he gleefully reported back to the *Orthodox Journal.*

Unfortunately in his numerous interviews with Cardinal Litta, Milner went a lot further, claiming the English Catholic clergy were 'sold to the laity' who were themselves 'enemies of Rome and without religion.' Finally, he accused Poynter of fraud by depriving him (Milner) of his share of the funds provided by the Papal Treasury. Cardinal Litta immediately wrote to Poynter asking for an explanation but as the letter never reached its destination, no answer reached Rome. This allowed Milner to add fuel to the fire for he told anyone who was prepared to listen that the lack of response it simply indicated his brother Bishop had no answer to make. Dr. Poynter, however, was not without friends at the Vatican and they made sure that he was eventually made aware of the allegations being made against him and on November 28 1814, despite the prospect of crossing the Alps in winter, he set out from London with the Rev. James Bramston[13] (soon to be his co-adjutor) for the long and arduous journey across Europe.

According to Ward the normal cost of a journey between London and Rome at this time, using carriages making regular journeys between the major towns and cities, was £35-£40, but the travelling expenses of Poynter and Bramston amounted to £197 because they hired a cabriolet in Paris to take them all the way to Rome, changing horses at various stages along the route. They left Paris on December 8, travelling via Fountainbleau, where they visited the Pope's apartments, then on through Dijon, Macon, Lyon, Savoy and Modane, crossing the snow-covered

Alps at Mont Cenis and arrived at Turin on Christmas Day. After resting for two days they set off once again, experiencing snow, rain and frost as they travelled down through Piacenza and Modena to Florence. At one point they had six oxen, as well as the normal four horses, pulling their cabriolet. After that the weather improved and the rest of the journey was free of further incident - apart from an earthquake that struck the little town of Radicolani, where they were spending the night - and they finally arrived in Rome on Saturday, 14 January. They were met a mile and a half outside the city by a carriage and pair, with coachman and footman, provided by the Pope for their use throughout their visit, which was to last three months. It is at this point that we can now return to our principal subject, for Ward reports:

> Several prominent Catholics were also in Rome, and paid their respects to Dr. Poynter, the chief being Sir Edward Blount, Mr George Silvertop, and a son of Lord Clifford.[14]

In his diary, the Rev. Bramston recorded that they met Silvertop the day after their arrival in Rome, on Sunday 15 January. No specific record has yet been discovered indicating when exactly the Squire of Minsteracres left England on this occasion, but the following chapter is to be devoted to what he had accomplished *en route* to the Eternal City, which would suggest that he most probably left home as soon after peace had been declared as bishops Milner and Poynter. What is clear, as we shall see, is that he travelled *via* Paris, raising the possibility that he was in the French capital at the same time as Poynter and met Castlereagh – or maybe later, in August, when the newly-elevated Duke of Wellington arrived in Paris to take up his appointment as British Ambassador. The significance of Silvertop meeting with either Castlereagh or Wellington, or both, in Paris will be explained later but in the meantime, so as to put his movements in their proper context, it is now necessary to summarize the situation across the Channel as peace returned, albeit briefly, to Europe.

The fall of Napoleon had sent many dignitaries on their travels again. The Russian Tsar, Alexander 1, and King William III of Prussia, for example, headed straight for London to celebrate their legitimacy with the Prince Regent; Louis XVIII, who had been granted asylum by the British, decided not to stay for the festivities and was already on his way back to Paris; the Spanish royal family were returning from detention in France and other minor rulers all over Europe were trying to reassemble the pattern of power that Napoleon's armies – and his habit of distributing domains to his relatives and supporters – had so grievously disrupted.[15] First came the Treaty of Fountainbleau (13 April 1814), the most important of its twenty-one articles allowing him to maintain the title of 'Emperor', giving him 'full sovereignty and property' over Elba, and a pension of two million francs a year. The Treaty of Paris followed two weeks later restoring Louis XVIII to his kingdom – not the vast empire that Napoleon had created, but the country of his ancestors, the pre-Revolutionary France of 1792. The gouty and corpulent Louis was to the people of France a stranger who had spent the last twenty years as a guest of their enemy, Great Britain. His Bourbon Charter promised to reverse the mistakes of his ancestors and guarantee liberalism but few of the French, in particular the peasants, had faith in this document. The general fear was that their land and their liberties would fall victim to the hordes of *émigré* aristocrats following in the king's wake. There was certainly unease and dissatisfaction among extreme Royalists and Bonapartists alike, an indication of trouble to come.

The overall future shape of Europe, meanwhile, was up for negotiation by the Allied Powers - at a special conference, the Congress of Vienna, which met for the first time in September 1814. It was said that the various sovereigns, their advisers, diplomats, ambassadors and courtiers, who gathered in the Austrian capital spent as much time in the beds of their mistresses and enjoying other delights the city had to offer as they did at the conference table. What is more, despite the need to maintain a united front against Napoleon, the negotiating Powers were at times closer to re-igniting war than securing the peace. Among the issues under discussion was one with direct links to Catholic emancipation in England and Ireland: those parts of the Papal States that had not already been restored. For months prior to the gathering in Vienna negotiations had been going on between the Foreign Secretary Lord Castlereagh and the Pope's special envoy, Cardinal Consalvi. Their first meeting had been in London, in the summer of 1814, when the Cardinal, showing commendable courage in approaching a land where for more than two centuries no cardinal had set foot, and where all diplomatic intercourse with the Holy See was prohibited, arrived bearing a letter from His Holiness. On the Continent, even in Protestant countries, Papal Legate was accorded precedence over all below the rank of royalty[16]but Consalvi behaved with great circumspection, putting aside the ordinary dress of a cardinal and appearing only in black. The result, according to Ward[17], was that Consalvi was received with civility and even cordiality during his visit. He and Castlereagh met again in Paris (during Poynter's visit, mentioned earlier) and then again in Vienna. According to Ward

Consalvi was so anxious to secure the good will of Great Britain in the Congress that he went to the furthest possible limits

106

in order to obtain it – farther in fact than was later accepted by the Pope.[18]

Despite all this goodwill there was still a long way to go for England's Catholics before they could celebrate their emancipation. And in the meantime, Napoleon and George Silvertop were destined to occupy centre stage once again, each in their own way.

References & Notes:

[1] Ward – Eve, vol.2, p. 189.

[2] An ill-disguised reference to Charles Butler and George Silvertop.

[3] John Milner, *Supplementary Memoirs*, pp.302-305.

[4] Leo Gooch, 'Catholic Biblemongers: Silvertop or Copperbottom?' *Northern Catholic History*, vol. 43, p.39.

[5] Marlow Sidney, from Cowpen Hall, reproduced an almost exact copy of this version in 1818.

[6] The first volume of his *History, Civil and Ecclesiastical, and Survey of the Antiquities of Winchester*, was published in 1798.

[7] H&B, p. 97.

[8] Ward – Eve, vol. 2, p. 88.

[9] F.C.Husenbeth, *Life of Milner*, James Duffy, Dublin, 1862.

[10] Ward-Eve, vol. .2, chapters XXII & XXIII.

[11] *Ibid*, vol. 2, p. 100.

[12] *Ibid.*

[13] Originally a Protestant and a lawyer, Bramston (1753-1836) went to the English College in Lisbon after his conversion and was made vicar general by Bishop Poynter in 1812 and coadjutor –Bishop in 1823.

[14] Ward Eve, vol. 2, p. 121.

[15] Norman Mackenzie, *The Fall and Flight of Napoleon 1814-1815*, Oxford University Press, 1982 (hereafter, Mackenzie).

[16] Neilsen, *Papacy in XIX Century*, I, p. 32.

[17] Ward –Eve, vol. 2, p. 92

[18] *Ibid*, vol.2, p. 132.

Chapter Seven

Face to face with Napoleon

Historians generally agree that it was never likely that Napoleon would settle for peaceful retirement in Elba. He was just forty three years of age, and if his energies were at a low ebb at the time of his abdication, a few months of rest restored him to his former mental vigour, to the extent that a tiny island nineteen miles long and sixty one wide could hardly hope to contain him. During his initial few months of exile he behaved more like a rich man taking a holiday in his newly acquired estate, but there was never enough to keep him occupied and he had ever-increasing financial problems. The Bourbon government showed no intention of honouring the financial terms of the Treaty of Fountainbleau and Napoleon's private funds depleted so fast that his beloved mother had to sell her jewels to pay his small army.[1] Of course, there were several reasons why it suited Napoleon to plead poverty but probably the most important was that the money he had been promised had become a symbol. If King Louis found he could ignore the financial clauses of the Treaty – which would clearly result in Napoleon's insolvency – then there was very little to stop the King of France flouting all other stipulations and treating Napoleon as an outlaw.[2]

Meanwhile, at the conference table in Vienna, British Foreign Secretary Castlereagh was receiving regular despatches from Colonel Neil Campbell, the British Army officer who had been appointed gaoler-cum-ambassador-to-Elba (without any official status), in which he described Napoleon's growing frustration as the weeks passed without any mention of his pension. 'I have been informed from good authority that his present funds are nearly exhausted,' Campbell reported in October. By mid-November he was linking Napoleon's need for money with a warning about his restless intentions.[3] Castlereagh had always made a distinction between fighting against Napoleon and fighting against France: his willingness to leave France with her pre-war boundaries reflected his desire to avoid humiliating the French. On the other hand, he had never trusted Napoleon and there was never any doubt in his mind that he would have to be defeated in the field.[4] So what made Napoleon decide to escape? Years later, in exile on the island of St Helena, he told his surgeon, Dr Barry O'Meara:

When I was at Elba, I was visited by an English nobleman, a Catholic, about thirty years old, and from Northumberland, I believe. He had dined a few weeks before with the Duke de Fleury, with whom he had a conversation relating to the sum of money to be allowed me annually by

110

France, according to the agreement of the Allied Powers. The Duke laughed at him for supposing for a moment that it would be complied with, and said that they were not such fools. *This was one of the reasons which induced me to quit Elba.* [Emphasis added].[5]

Unfortunately, Napoleon's memory seems to have played tricks on him on this occasion, conveniently merging, in the mists of time, two visitors into one. First, the 'English nobleman ... about thirty years old' we can now reveal, was Viscount Ebrington (1783-1861) while, secondly, the 'Catholic ...from Northumberland' was George Silvertop. From his own record of the event, entitled *1814: Memoranda on visits to Napoleon*[6] we know that Ebrington had two meetings with Napoleon – the first on 6 December, then again at dinner two days later – and as Napoleon told Silvertop he had been introduced to Ebrington 'two days earlier'[7] his meeting with the Emperor must have taken place during the day on 8 December.

Bramston, in his diary, recording the fact that he and Poynter had dined with Silvertop in Rome on 18 January (1815), adds briefly 'Interesting account he gave of his visit to Elba', but the only full, first-hand account of the occasion is said to have been in a letter he (Silvertop) was prompted to write to his friend Charles Butler some eight years later. (See

111

Appendix 2). The original letter sadly no longer exists, but Butler does refer to it in the fourth edition of his *Reminiscences*[8] published in 1824, in a note, introducing what he describes as 'an important portion' of 'a highly interesting conversation which the Emperor held at Elba with a friend.' This clearly edited version of the letter, however, makes no mention of Napoleon's pension – or of the Duke de Fleury. It is worth noting here that it was a year earlier (1823) that O'Meara published his book containing Napoleon's comments and some sixty years later (1888) that Richard Welford published his biography of the Squire of Minsteracres, which included the following statement:

> In the course of their chat, the question of the pension guaranteed to the exile out of the revenues of France was mentioned, and Mr Silvertop was able to inform his host that, only a few days earlier the Duke de Fleury, with whom he had dined in Paris, had scoffed at the idea that the French Government would observe the financial part of the Treaty, and expressed a confident opinion that they were not such fools.

This is rather different, however, to the version used by the Rev. George Silvertop a hundred years after the event in his *Memoirs of the Silvertops*. He gives the impression of having seen

112

the original letter, for he records the fact that the squire was asked by Butler to set down his recollection of their conversation, and provides this version of the reference to the Emperor's pension:

> He (Napoleon) then turned to the Congress of Vienna, said he suspected they were plotting against Naples, and even against him in his miserable island. To this I replied that I was perfectly ignorant, but that I had been informed by a person in a high situation in the French Government, that the money agreed to be paid to His Majesty, would be discontinued. He said, it was very likely – already they had not performed their stipulation.

In a brief note at the bottom of the page, the Rev. Silvertop says, 'This statement is probably what O'Meara refers to.' To add to the confusion caused by the different versions, Butler's reference highlights mention of the execution of Duke d'Engheim, which Napoleon apparently blamed on Prince Talleyrand[9], but this does not appear in any other of the versions. Then the Squire of Ministeracres himself, does admit to Butler that his letter represents only 'the *greater part* [emphasis added] of the conversation I had the honour to have with the Emperor Napoleon, many particulars of which, on my return from the Continent, some years ago, I communicated to you.' In his *Memoirs* years later, the Rev. Lenders[10] added something else, which appears in no other version - that Napoleon presented Silvertop with a framed mosaic picture, representing an angel, which for many years, according to Lenders, hung on the landing leading to the Chapel passage on the first floor at Minsteracres.

Bonaparte, of course, had many visitors during his 100 days on the island - English and otherwise, including a number of his own informants and spies from the mainland - and we shall probably now never know who it was that dined with the Duke de Fleury, although it would seem it was neither Silvertop or Ebrington, who in his 69-page memoranda[11] on his meetings with Napoleon, dismisses their conversations as 'desultory' and makes no reference to the Duke de Fleury or Napoleon's pension.

According to Norman MacKenzie's account of the escape[12], 'an unidentified messenger arrived at Portoferraio (Elba's capital) on 6 December' and one of Napoleon's more experienced spies is said to have written in his journal: 'From that day His Majesty's character altered. His words were few and he seemed morose and abstracted.' A few weeks earlier, during a four-hour discussion with another English visitor, George W. Vernon, a Whig MP who was a cousin of Lord Holland, Napoleon had shrugged off any responsibility for any trouble brewing in France with the words:

'That doesn't concern me. I am like a dead man, my role is finished.'[13]

It obviously suited Napoleon to have a succession of well-connected Englishmen visiting him on Elba. Lacking any kind of diplomatic recognition except Campbell's ambiguous appointment, he thought their attentions improved his standing generally and from the moment he asked Castlereagh for asylum in England, he had clung to the bizarre notion that the English might be willing to offer him a more congenial home than Elba. However, he was astute enough never to miss an opportunity to elicit information that could be useful should he decide to quit Elba. Frequently walking up and down, jumping from one topic to another, he would carefully quiz them about the political situation in England, or the impression they had formed as they travelled through France and Italy, and when he expressed his opinion he watched closely to see how they reacted.

This is the way it was with George Silvertop and we have seen nothing so far to exclude the possibility that it was the Squire of Minsteracres that dined with the Duke de Fleury and, perhaps more intriguingly, that he was put up to visiting Elba by either Castlereagh or Wellington, or both, with the object of adding flames to Napoleon's anxieties over his finances. As it happened, it was only a matter of days before Castlereagh was being blamed for organising Napoleon's escape so that he could be dealt a final blow by

Wellington. In a report to the Austrian Secret Service one informed claimed:

> There are those who believe that the English have allowed him to escape in order to recapture him or to have an excuse for treating him with the utmost severity ...others say that it was not an escape but a departure arranged by the English.[14]

It had taken almost two weeks for the news to reach Vienna and caused such confusion that newspapers were forbidden to report the event for several days while the sovereigns and their ministers considered what to do. The Emperor's escape had an equally disturbing effect in Naples, where Napoleon's brother-in-law, Joachim Murat, the self-styled King of Naples, is said to have exploded with scarcely controlled excitement at the news. MacKenzie reports: 'Like an old warhorse pricking its ears at the sound of a distant trumpet, he was keen for action and for glory – the seductive combination of vanity and power that drove Napoleon himself, and possessed almost everyone who served under him.'[15] Consequently it was not long before Murat was on the march with his army on what turned out to be a totally disastrous campaign against the Austrians.

George Silvertop, meanwhile, had arrived in Italy and after a stay in Rome during which he had his first private audience with Pope Pius VII[16]; he travelled on to Naples. There is no detailed account of his meeting with Napoleon's brother-in-law, but we learn from a letter he is said to have written from Florence a few weeks later, that he had become increasingly concerned by what he had heard while visiting the court of the self-styled King of Naples.

> The moment I got out of my carriage (on arriving back in Rome) I went to Cardinal Litta. I told him I was persuaded the Pope was in great danger from the Court of Naples, having heard the King, as well as several generals, speak on the subject of the Pope and his cardinals, and earnestly entreated him as a British subject, as a Catholic and as a man, to finish the business which could be done that evening. His answer was we are in the Holy Week, we are all bustle and confusion. In two days afterwards the Pope left Rome with Litta and all his cardinals except Fesch.

Silvertop said the Pope and his party travelled to Florence, then to Livorno *en route* to Genoa (probably because it was under British control at the time). 'The Pope is to be carried for 30 miles on men's shoulders over the mountains between Lirice and Genoa,' he said, adding darkly: 'Thus stands our affair with the Court of Rome.' [17]

This so-called letter, dated Florence, 31 March 1815, is fascinating for a number of reasons. Firstly, it is headed *Extracts of Letters from Mr Silvertop*, with no clue as to the intended recipient, it is hand-written (though, comparing the writing with others in existence, not by Silvertop himself) and is unsigned. Secondly, it would appear to be an assessment of the discussions Dr. Poynter and the Rev. Bramston were having in Rome, and, finally, the writer implies he is travelling with someone else, though he does not identify his companion. The extract, which is included in a bundle of correspondence held by Cambridge University Library – the others are all original letters written by Silvertop to his friend Lingard, at a much later date – begins:

Permit me to observe that no two men would have taken more pains or conducted their negotiations with more wisdom than Dr. Poynter and Mr Bramston. After refuting prejudices and disproving most victoriously assertions made by Dr. Milner; & when Dr. Poynter stood in the eyes of Cardinal Litta as an honest man, he delivered in his project to the Pope in person, as well as to Cardinal Litta. It is founded on the principle of the loyalty of persons exercising Episcopal functions being approved of by the Crown previous to there being invested with spiritual functions. This proposition met with universal approbation – nor is it surprising that it should do so for a most able document, more clear and better calculated to render great and essential service I never perused.[18] I fancy I hear you say, but why then did the Pope not adopt it? To this I can only answer to you, the cause arises from the disgusting, the puerile dilatoriness of the Court of Rome.

He says that Poynter and Bramston 'left Rome before we did' but had not yet arrived in Florence, having probably followed His Holiness to Livorno. He then goes on:

> Our Ecclesiastical affairs were to have been settled next Monday in the Congregation and no doubt seems to exist but that everything wished would have been settled to our satisfaction. With respect to Quarantotti's letter, it is true that the Pope called it to himself; that prevented its being discussed, till he thought proper it should be discussed and sentence pronounced upon it. Nothing has been done since it was in his hands and the letter remains in all its force, as the letter of his Vice regent vested with full authority during his absence. I can most positively state that not only the Pope, but Cardinals Litta etc. have assured me that it is not

only desirable but that it is right and wise, that the loyalty of persons called to exercise Episcopal functions should be fully approved by governments prior to their receiving spiritual jurisdiction and I am persuaded from their assertions that they wish the Parliament of G.B. to legislate without our consulting them on the subject. That every thing would have been done, I really believe, if things had remained quiet, & may be possible, though probably not in their confusion, be done in Genoa. The dilatoriness of the Court of Rome is proverbial and it is perhaps not much to be wondered at that a Vicar Apostolic and his Vicar (presumably Dr. Poynter and Mr. Bramston) could not obtain dispatch, when a French Ambassador with an immense suit of able men, backed by all the power of the King, could after nine months labour, procure not one object of his embassy. That amiable man, the Bishop of St. Malo, is here and laments with myself the dilatory and puerile conduct.

Now, if we were to consider that this 'extract' was in fact a report, rather than a private letter, it would perhaps help to explain another intriguing anecdote associated with George Silvertop that first came to light in his obituary, published in the *Gateshead Observer* on 24 February, 1849. After recording his visit to Elba and his conversation with Napoleon, the obituary went on:

> Shortly afterwards, in consequence of his (Silvertop's) reputation as a man of high character and ability, he was selected by Lord Liverpool's Cabinet as the medium of private communication between Great Britain and the See of Rome, on matters affecting the conditions of British Roman Catholics. Although the negotiation was unproductive of satisfactory results, Mr. Silvertop acquitted himself of his difficult and delicate trust with acknowledged talent and address.

The anonymous author of the obituary offered no further details – let alone a source – to authenticate this claim, and a current search of all possible avenues has failed to confirm or deny the report, yet every biographical mention of George Silvertop since that date has attributed him with this 'secret mission'. Authentication dating back to 1815, it has to be acknowledged, is unlikely ever to have existed, given that emancipation was still many years away and official contact between the government and Catholics would have been considered unthinkable. Furthermore, Daniel O'Connell[19], leader of the popular party in Ireland, had already been stirring up a storm about alleged secret negotiations between the Liverpool

Government and the Catholic laity in England on the question of the veto.

On the other hand, George Silvertop survived for twenty years after the Emancipation Act was finally passed in 1929 and one must assume that someone in-the-know provided justification for the comment in his obituary that he had 'acquitted himself ... with acknowledged talent and address.' The only problem is that we are reasonably certain that he did not visit Rome again until 1820 and anyway, although the Catholic question came before Parliament year after year – to be defeated on all occasions - the five years following his first visit covered a period dominated mostly by domestic affairs. Some confusion could be attributed to the words 'Upon his return ...' included in Welford's version of events, but taking a clue from the words 'Shortly afterwards' used in the obituary, there is another possibility, which we can examine by introducing three other recent arrivals in Italy at that time, all of whom were there as a direct consequence of events unfolding in Europe at the time.

The first was Lord William Bentinck (1774-1839) who was in charge of the British forces protecting Ferdinand I in Sicily and in early 1814 had occupied Genoa. He had met the Pope on his way back to Rome after being released by Napoleon and, finding him in a state of penury, had lent him four thousand crowns of British Secret Service money to help him re-establish himself.[20] Why His Lordship should be carrying British Secret Service money is a fascinating question but sadly unrelated to our story as there is no evidence to suggest that he met Silvertop on this or any other occasion. The next to arrive was the elegant Lord Burghersh (1784-1859) later the tenth Duke of Westmorland, whose family home was Raby Castle, County Durham, and whose ancestors built Brancepeth Castle. A distinguished army officer who had served in the Napoleonic Wars, he was British military commissioner with the allies in Paris when Wellington arrived as Ambassador. Two months later (October) Burghersh was on his way to Florence as the British Envoy to the Tuscan Government and (possibly indicating his top priority) he was soon complaining that its police at Livorno and Piombino – the two ports serving Elba –were so bad that the number of persons 'who pass through this state to Elba, and return without being known to the Government, is very great.'[21]We know that Silvertop spent some time in Florence and is almost certain to have known Burghersh from County Durham and therefore it seems fair to assume that they met, although we have no proof.

The last man to arrive was Edward Cooke, an under-secretary at the Foreign Office with considerable experience of confidential missions. English by birth and educated at Eton and Cambridge, he had lived for many years in Ireland and at the time of the Union had taken a prominent part on the side of the English Government; but he had looked upon Catholic emancipation as an integral part of the scheme, which he consequently considered to have been only partially carried through.[22] Quiet and unobtrusive, Cooke was a close personal friend of Lord Castlereagh, had been with the Foreign Secretary at the negotiations in Vienna, and had been despatched to Rome just four days before news reached the Austrian capital of Napoleon's escape. In Rome Bramston made the following entry in his diary on 22 January 22:

> Intrigue evident I think!!!. Silvertop came in – had a conversation with Mr Cooke – read part of the paper delivered to Cardinal Litta – was very thankful.[23]

Now, given the highly-charged atmosphere created by Napoleon's subsequent escape and Murat's march on Austria – under the very noses of the Great Powers gathered in Vienna – reliable intelligence would have been at a premium (as confirmed by documents held at Nottingham University Library[24]) and the Squire of Minsteracres quite possibly found himself in the right place, at the right time and with the right contacts, to be of some help.

Regrettably, it seems, we may never know the full story.

References & Notes:

[1] Robin Neillands, *Wellington and Napoleon,* John Murray, 1994.

[2] Mackenzie, p. 172

[3] *Ibid,* p. 172.

[4] John W. Derry, *Castlereagh,* Allen Lane, 1976.

[5] Barry E. O'Meara, *A Voice from St. Helena,* London, 1823.

[6] *1814: memorandum on visits to Napoleon,* Oxford University, Ref. MS. Eng. Misc. e 605.

[7] See full text at *Appendix 1.*

[8] Charles Butler, *Reminiscences,* John Murray: London, 1824, pp. 163-166.

[9] Former Bishop, appointed Foreign Minister 1797; Napoleon supporter until 1807, thereafter much involved in political intrigue. Became organiser of Provisional Government in 1814.

[10] The Rev. Jules Lenders was chaplain at Minsteracres, 1922-1928.

[11] Oxford Bodleian Library, MSS.Eng.misc.e.605.

[12] Mackenzie, p.154.

[13] *Ibid,* p .142

[14] *Ibid,* p. 239.

[15] *Ibid,* p. 241.

[16] It was during a speech in Newcastle years later (1826) that Silvertop revealed he had been granted an audience by the Pope on that occasion and later had two further meetings.

[17] Cambridge University Library. Add. MSS 9418/15/75.

[18] A copy of the original document produced by Dr. Poynter, hand-written, signed and dated February 18, 1815, exists in the National Archives in Kew, ref: F04.3/7.

[19] Daniel O'Connell (1775-1847) was at Douay in 1792, entered Lincoln's Inn in 1794 and returned to Ireland in 1798.

[20] Mackenzie, p. 115.

[21] Ibid, p. 148.

[22] Ward –Eve, p. 127.

[23] Westminster Diocesan Archives, SEC 15:3/8

[24] Correspondence involving Lord Bentinck, Lord Burghersh, Edward Cooke and others, Nottingham University Library, MSS PwJd 1723/ PwJd 5437/PwJd 5439-31/PwJd 5443.

George Silvertop

Published by kind permission of Ms Veronica Silvertop

Chapter Eight

Milner is finally gagged

We have no record to suggest when Silvertop returned from Italy that year: one of the more fanciful anecdotes surrounding this particular member of the family suggests he was actually at Waterloo at the time of the battle, but there is no evidence to support this. More reliably, he was reported to be still in Florence when Poynter, now totally vindicated, left with Bramston on 28 April, travelling first to Venice and then *via* the Brenner Pass, through Munich, Stuttgardt, Frankfurt and Cologne, so as to avoid France. They passed through Brussels on 6 June – twelve days before the Battle of Waterloo – and arrived back at Dover four days later. Milner had returned some months earlier, with little to show for his year abroad apart from a diminished reputation in Rome, but unrepentant nonetheless; his passionate and impulsive behaviour, his random statements, meaningless retractions and reckless grasp at any missile to fling at an opponent were to continue – for the moment – unabated. And very soon it was to be George Silvertop who would attract his undivided attention.

At Christmas 1815 the Squire was back home celebrating the yuletide with his mother, who was still very much the Mistress of Minsteracres at seventy years of age, but it is likely to have been the recent events in France that were dominating his thoughts. The principal purpose of his visit to the north that Christmas was to chair a meeting drawing attention to religious rioting in the south of France and to protest at the brutal way it had been put down by the authorities. What he did not expect was that, thanks to Milner and the *Orthodox Journal*, it was to dramatically raise his public profile nationwide. The rioting had flared between the Huguenots and Catholics in the aftermath of Napoleon's return and subsequent defeat at Waterloo. The Huguenots had always been allied to the Bonapartists and the ill feeling turned to rioting with the restoration of the Bourbons. Reports of the numbers killed – mostly Huguenots - varied wildly and the French Government were accused of having acquiesced in their massacre. Agitation continued in England for some months – a deputation was sent to the Prince Regent calling on him to make a stand for religious tolerance – until finally a letter arrived from Wellington, still Ambassador in Paris, declaring the whole incident had been exaggerated.

It was still, however, too good an opportunity for George Silvertop to miss, for it struck at the very heart of his beliefs. Following the example of the Irish, led by O'Connell, the ever increasingly popular gentleman of Kerry, who had already called for an end to all persecution, Silvertop chaired a packed meeting of Catholics in the Newcastle Assembly Rooms two days after Christmas, 1815. The eleven-point resolution Silvertop put to the meeting, however, went much further than the Irish and was couched in stronger language. While declaring allegiance to 'the sacred cause of Religious Freedom' it called for an end to the persecution of Protestants in France and promised that

> If our hopes shall be disappointed … we shall consider ourselves called upon by every principle of Christian charity and benevolence, to co-operate with our Protestant countrymen in extending to the Protestants of France, the same relief and assistance which, under similar circumstances, we should be ready to afford to persons of our own persuasion.

The resolution went on to say that 'contemplating the misfortunes of our fellow men, nature forces upon us the melancholy idea of our own degradation' and called upon the chairman to convey the views of the meeting to the Government.[1] It was just what Bishop Milner needed to return to the attack. As outlined by the Rev. Peter Phillips [2] the meeting received full coverage in the *Orthodox Journal* in a rather inflammatory report provided by Eusebius Andrews himself.[3] Andrews set the discussion in the context of the recent 'phrenetic disease, called the Biblemania', prompted no doubt by Silvertop's opening remarks expressing

> His anxious and sincere hope that education and science, and scriptural knowledge might spread themselves over the regions of the earth, and that mankind might learn from such inestimable resources, that liberty of conscience is the inalienable right of all.

Ward, writing much earlier, considered this remark if not in itself unorthodox, at any rate more suitable in the mouth of a Protestant than a Catholic.[4] Milner and Andrews of course, were at the time aghast and enthusiastically fuelled a controversy that continued in the pages of the *Orthodox Journal* from January that year to August 1816, filling more than fifty pages. Among the letter-writers was a Northumberland priest who wrote to defend Squire Silvertop in a long and carefully argued letter about religious freedom, defining his terms by way of Edward Hawarden's *Rule of Faith Truly Stated* (1721).[5] Hawarden, professor of theology at Douay at the beginning of the eighteenth century and falsely accused of Jansenist[6] leanings, was a significant figure in the attempts at refining the self-definition of late eighteenth century English Catholicism. It was a matter of steering a fine course between an unbounded assertion of the rights of private judgement, which no Catholic would be prepared to accept, and a way of upholding a reasonable submission to Church authority. Silvertop and other members of the Catholic Board were searching for a way towards an expression of this position and the Northumberland priest provided good grounds for doing just that. Milner, not surprisingly, was having none of it. Under the pseudonym *'Consistency'* he identified the writer as Rutter, George Silvertop's very own chaplain at Minsteracres. Whether Milner was right in his identification, we have no way of knowing (Phillips suggests in his article that perhaps Andrews had betrayed the author's anonymity). In any event, Milner dismissed the argument with a typical trenchant rhetorical flourish, penned as the imaginary words of Rutter's uncle, Banister, long-since dead:

> The writer's illustrious uncle would not have applauded this among his publications, but rather would have

sternly said to him; H—y, when thou writest in the cause of true Religion, spare no false doctrine, or profane novelty, whether it is broached by a friend or a stranger, whether by a Mr SILVERTOP or a Mr COPPER-BOTTOM. And, after all, what signifies, H—y, thy perverting the meaning of our master Hawarden, to gloss over latitudinarian decisions passed by fox-hunting laymen, amidst the orgies of Bacchus; when thou knowest well it is the practice of the Catholic Church to qualify propositions IN SENSU AUCTORIS, and when it appears, from thy friend's speech, as well as from his Resolutions, that he thinks (or at least that he thought so at the Tavern in Newcastle) all articles of religious belief to rest upon private opinion, and that every individual, whether Protestant or Pagan, has the same natural and even SACRED (that is to say, DIVINE) right to believe his Religion to be the true one, as thou hast to believe this to be so.

Just a few pages later in the same issue of the *Orthodox*, Milner returned to the attack on the Catholic Board's Bible. In another letter, this time signed 'Col. Ang. Duac. Alum', he declared the Board's New Testament had been 'falsely published' and suggested a more appropriate title page:

A Liberal and Gentlemanlike Edition of the
New Testament in English, for
enlightening the Catholic Poor, to frame
their own religion by the bare text of it,
published at the desire of certain
Protestant Biblemen by -.

In addition, Bishop Milner issued a letter to his
clergy condemning the Newcastle resolutions:

It is not the Catholic rule of faith that every
individual should judge of the
reasonableness of every article of his faith,
but he is to believe them on the authority
of the Catholic Church.

Nevertheless, as recorded by Mons.Ward, many
of the Catholic clergy considered that the sense
attributed by Milner was not necessarily
attachable to the words of the resolutions. They
contended that those words were not
incompatible with the profession of belief in an
infallible teaching Church, and only asserted the
right to judge of the reasons for that belief – that
is, in theological language, of the "*motiva
credibilitatis!*" [7] In any event, it seems incredible
that a Bishop should be allowed to continue to
behave with such lack of dignity and in such an
intemperate manner, but as John Lingard,
another of his favourite victims, was to write
some time later

I am not surprised that Dr Milner has acted as he has done. Though he affects so much independence, the fact is, I suspect, that his conduct has placed him in a situation in which he has none. He has dwindled into a mere tool of the Irish bishops.[8]

Lingard at this time was out of the country, having accepted an invitation from Lord Stourton (his former pupil and companion on his escape from Douay, who had succeeded to the title the year before) to accompany him and his family on a Grand Tour. But even then he was not entirely free of Milner's vitriol. One of Lingard's principal reasons for accepting the invitation was so that once they reached Rome he would be able to consult the manuscripts stored in the Vatican archives as part of his research into English history, but when he arrived in the Holy City he found Cardinal Litta, who was in charge at that time of anything to do with the English Mission, 'civil but extremely cool.' According to Ward, Milner had written to Litta cautioning him against anything Lingard might say, urging that Lingard's work should be discouraged.[9]

On returning from a trip to Naples, however, Lingard appealed to Secretary of State Cardinal Consalvi, who immediately sent for the man in charge of the archives and 'told him to order, in his name, all the officers to give me every facility, and to procure for me such manuscripts as I should then mark down in writing.'[10] Consequently Lingard returned to England in the autumn of 1817 with sufficient material from the archives of Rome, Milan and Paris, to complete the first three volumes of his *History of England*. He offered the book to two Catholic publishers in London - one declined it out of hand while the other, Booker of Bond Street, offered him £300 for the copyright, which Lingard considered inadequate and turned to his friend, George Silvertop who had always encouraged him in his literary efforts for help. Silvertop took the manuscript to a publisher called Mawman, at Ludgate Hill, London, who at first was less than enthusiastic, saying that history was a poor thing on which to speculate. By coincidence, however, Mawman had a visit from Lord Holland, a former Ambassador to Florence who became a convert to Catholicism, and Mawman happened to mention that he had been sent a new history, to which Holland remarked that he knew of only one man who could write such a book – Lingard. 'Why,' said Mawman, 'that is the name of the author?' The manuscript was lent to Holland, considered a man of great literary judgement, who gave it his unqualified approval[11] and so on 17 March 1818, Silvertop wrote from his London hotel:

My dear Lingard - I am happy to inform you that I have this day concluded the

Bargain with Mr Mawman (a Newcastle publisher) for your manuscript, or rather the copyright of the 'History of England', for £1,000. He desires me to say he will have great pleasure in presenting you with some copies, in order to enable you to make presents to some friends. I have in his name to propose to you (what to me I must say seems very fair) another £1,000 for the second part of your History, provided it contains as much matter as that for which he has enjoyed, and £500 more if he gives a new edition of the present manuscript before your second part is ready for the Press. To this I must have an answer by return of Post, as I leave London on Tuesday next and if you assent to it, I think you may fairly add that you expect something in addition if your second part goes to a second edition. There are many things respecting your work I wish to see you upon and therefore will make a point of going to Lartington (his brother's home at Barnard Castle) where I hope to go in April or May and where I hope you will meet me. I shall take care to bring the manuscript with me.[12]

When the agreement was signed Lingard had written only up to the end of the reign Edward II, but by the time the three volumes went to press the following October he had revised all that he had already written, made numerous additions, and added the reigns of the succeeding monarchs up to and including Henry VII. 'This I did,' he subsequently wrote, 'so as not to stop the press an hour; but it was a greater labour than I ever underwent in my life; nor would I have done it, had I not found that unless I fixed a time I should never get through. Hence, I attended little to style.'[13] [In 1820 the reigns of Henry VIII and Edward VI appeared in a fourth volume; those of Mary, Elizabeth, James I, Charles I and Charles II followed at various intervals, and in the spring of 1830, the eighth and concluding volume brought Lingard's *History* up to the Revolution of 1688]. At home and on the Continent the work was greeted with admiration by scholars of every creed and in 1821 Pope Pius VII conferred on him the triple academic laurels and created him doctor of divinity and of canon and civil law. The work went through five editions in England in Lingard's lifetime, not to mention the American editions and also one published from Galignani's celebrated pres in Paris.[14]

The story of Lingard's *History* would not be complete, however, without recording Milner's reaction. According to Ward, Lingard's colourless and unimpassioned style of writing was unintelligible to Milner, who considered the appearance of such a work as a golden opportunity to enforce the Catholic aspect of English history, and he looked upon Lingard as having betrayed the cause.[15] Ironically it was

Milner's bitter criticism of Lingard's work that would lead ultimately, not only to his own gagging, but also to the demise of the *Orthodox Journal*, the vehicle of much of his vitriol. His first salvo against the *History* appeared soon after its publication in a letter to the *Journal* bearing the initials '*J.M.*' which began:

Mr Editor – Calumniated, misrepresented and ridiculed as our Holy religion, the original Christianity of this and every other country which professes the name of Jesus, is and long has been by our ignorant or bigoted countrymen, it is a deplorable misfortune that since the days of Bishop Challoner and Alban Butler, most of the individuals of our body, whom God has qualified to vindicate it, should aid or at least connive at those irreligious acts against it.

After a few words against his favourite 'victims', such as Charles Butler and the Rev. Joseph Berington[16], Milner went on:

I am far, Mr Editor, from placing a late Catholic historian in the same list with the above mentioned betrayers of their religion; were I to do this I should act in opposition to my judgement as well as to my sentiments; for few individuals are more interested in thinking favourably of him than myself; but this I say, and I say it in unison with all Catholics of my acquaintance, who sincerely venerate and love their religion, he has not filled the expectations we had formed of his work: he has not done justice to his own abilities and learning any more than to the victorious merits of his subject: he has not sufficiently refuted the calumnies nor dissipated the misrepresentations of a Bale, a Barker, a Godwin, an Echard, a Hulme, a Smollett, a Littleton, a Goldsmith, and a score more of Protestant or infidel writers; nor has he displayed the beauty of holiness irradiating the doctrine and heroes of Catholicity, in the manner that he might have done. In short, the 'History of England' that has lately appeared from the shop of Mawman in Ludgate Street, is not a Catholic history, such as our calumniated and depressed condition calls for.

Milner went on to complain that the appellation 'Saint' had not been prefixed to those generally known to Catholics, such as Augustine, Gregory, Thomas a'Becket etc. and, highlighting Lingard's treatment of St. Thomas, summed up by saying: 'If this, Mr Editor, is not sacrificing the cause of the Church in the person of one of its canonised martyrs ... I know not what is.'

Lingard, as was his custom, took no notice of the letter, even when Milner proceeded to write to the Irish bishops, begging them to join him in discrediting the book – and he later tried to obtain an adverse verdict in Rome. Neither attempt succeeded, and eventually, in the autumn of 1819, that which many people had been waiting for, actually occurred: Milner fell out with the proprietor/editor of the *Journal*[17]. It was initially over a letter signed 'Candidus'[18] which appeared in the *Journal* defending Lingard's *History*. Milner argued that a letter containing such views should never have been published; Andrews responded by attacking Milner, describing one of his pastoral letters as a 'political circular.' Furious, Milner hit back by declaring he would never again write for the *Journal*. Whether or not he would have kept his resolution we will never know for the following Spring (1820) the Catholic Board decided to send George Silvertop and his mentor, Henry Howard of Corby, to Rome to present a formal complaint against Milner's writings, taking with them a collection of extracts from the *Journal*. Howard's diaries covering this period - described by Gillow as being 'of considerable historical importance'[19]- sadly no longer exist, but we know that after due consideration, and with the Pope's authority, Milner was told he would be stripped of his vicariate if he wrote for the *Journal* again. And as if to add insult to injury, the letter was sent to Dr Poynter, who was told to read it and then pass it on to his fellow bishop. The most important part of the letter read:

Scarcely are we able to persuade ourselves how a Vicar Apolstolic, bound by such close ties to the Holy See and the Sacred Congregation, can dare to forget his own ministry and spread abroad the seeds of discord, to trample upon the honour of high dignitaries who by their piety, learning and office shine pre-eminent among the clergy, and to incite the Catholic people against nobles of high birth, who not less for their rank than for the generosity with which they support the missions, deserve to be treated with all honour and respect. This does not proceed from zeal, as your Lordship may easily represent to yourself, but from a certain restless spirit of calumny and abuse, from which dissensions and other grave evils proceed; for as St. James teaches (iii 16) 'Where envying and contention is, there is inconstancy and every evil work' ...The interests of religion therefore, the dignity of the Holy See and the peace of Catholics demand the uprooting of this seed of discord, and inasmuch as in England the press is free, and that disgraceful journal cannot be suppressed, His Holiness wills, and in virtue of obedience due to the Supreme Head of the Church commands and orders your Lordship to take no further part henceforward, directly or indirectly, in the said journal, not to patronise or promote it in any way whatsoever, not to furnish it with material or arguments, and far less with any contribution. I doubt not that your Lordship will render prompt and full obedience to the command of our most holy Lord; lest in the event of disobedience he should be forced to withdraw your faculties and remove you from your office as Vicar.[20]

Milner, naturally, answered in his usual spirited style, declaring that his writings in the *Journal* had always been in defence of the rights of the Holy See but his appeal went unanswered and as for the *Journal*, without Milner's controversial contributions it withered and final died that same year. It was characteristic of Lingard that the only recorded reference in his correspondence to the silencing and humbling of his great antagonist, occurs in a letter written after the publication of his second volume of *History* – that he heard of no censures on his work, '…as there is no Orthodox now for Dr. Milner to write in.'[21] Milner was still very much on his mind, however, upon publication of the fifth volume of his work in 1823 for in a letter to Dr Poynter, Lingard wrote:

Mr Mawman tells me that Dr Milner will certainly attack me. I suspect I frightened him before: and I hope I do so again by spreading a report that I mean to retaliate.[22]

Dr Milner in fact refrained from publishing any criticism in England but his animosity was undiminished, for he directed his complaints to Rome, pleading for the Lingard's work to be censured. He was ignored and not long afterwards he died (1826). On his deathbed he expressed regret for his intemperate language – but did not retract or admit his calumnies.[23]

Meanwhile, the *Journal's* demise - it was later revived more than once, but it never succeeded long enough to become permanent – signalled the end of an era for English Catholics, but we should not lose sight of the fact that all of this was taking place against a background of general distress, discontent and political agitation. Hopes that the end of the long war with France would bring security and prosperity were dashed by the severe slump that came instead. The sudden end to demand for armaments and war materials like uniforms and boots threw many miners, iron and factory workers out of work to join the thousands of discharged soldiers and soldiers who were already struggling to find jobs. Agricultural workers joined the jobless queues when a sharp fall in wheat in 1814 and 1815 ruined thousands of farmers, causing a general shortage of food. A report in the *Newcastle Chronicle* in November 1816 claiming there were 112 families in Swalwell (south of the Tyne, not far from Stella) whose average weekly resources, including parish relief, amounted to no more than 1s. 10d. a head, gives an indication of what the poorer classes were having to cope with, when the cost of a small loaf of bread was one shilling.[24] The mayor and corporation of Newcastle opened soup kitchens and started a relief fund, but such measures did little more than alleviate the general privation and it was not long before the jobless and hungry mobs resorted to violence.

References & Notes:

[1] *Newcastle Chronicle,* Saturday December 30, 1815.

[2] Rev. Peter Phillips, *Catholic Biblemongers: Silvertop or Copperbottom?* Northern Catholic History, vol. 43, 2002, pp. 39-46.

[3] *Orthodox Journal*, January 1816, pp. 57-60.

[4] Ward – Eve, vol. 2, p. 238.

[5] *Orthodox Journal*, February 1816, pp. 57-60.

[6] Jansenism, emphasizing the more predestinatory approach of Augustine's teaching, divided the Roman Catholic Church in France in the mid seventeenth century. Jansenists were excommunicated in 1719.

[7] Ward - Eve, vol. 2, p. 238.

[8] H&B.

[9] Ward – Eve, vol. 2, p. 279.

[10] H&B, p.152.

[11] Gillow, pp. 254 – 272.

[12] Cambridge University Library, Add. Mss 9418/15/62.

[13] Gillow, p. 261.

[14] *Ibid.*

[15] Ward – Eve, vol. 2, p. 277.

[16] Author with Dr. Kirk of a tract published in 1813 entitled *Faith of Catholics*, much maligned by Milner.

[17] William Eusebius Andrews (1773-1837) was the son of Catholic converts of humble station. He began his newspaper career as an apprentice at the Norfolk Chronicle and rose to be editor (1799-1813). In 1813 he went to London to devote himself to advancing the Catholic cause by means of the press and in July that year established the *Orthodox Journal.*

[18] Milner's biographer says it was 'understood to be the Rev. John Fletcher.'

[19] Gillow, p.433.

[20] Ward – Eve, vol. 2, p. 187.

[21] H&B, p.180.

[22] *Ibid*, p. 199.

[23] David Mathew, *Catholicism in England (1535-1935),* Longmans, Green & Co., 1926, p. 166.

[24] S. Middlebrook, *Newcastle Upon Tyne, Its Growth and Achievement,* Newcastle, 1950, p.170.

George Silvertop

As featured in the Rev. Lenders' *Memoirs.*
The whereabouts of the original is unknown.

Henry (Silvertop) Witham

George Silvertop's younger brother, as
featured by the Rev. Lenders in his *Memoirs*.
The whereabouts of the original is unknown.

Lartington Hall
nr. Barnard Castle

The home of George Silvertop's
brother Henry Witham during
his lifetime, it was originally
part of the Maire estates, which
passed to the Lawson family
and finally to the Silvertops'
mother Catherine, known as
Mrs Silvertop Maire

Mrs Silvertop Maire

George Silvertop's mother, formerly
Catherine Lawson, who lived
on at Minsteracres for thirty years after
her husband died.

Chapter Nine

Behind the scenes

Social reform became the burning issue throughout the country for the next decade, spearheaded by activists calling themselves Political Protestants and culminating in the massacre of 'Peterloo' – a sad parody of Wellington's victory at Waterloo. Spawned by the common struggle for basic survival, reform societies sprang up in the north east, as elsewhere, not only in larger towns like Newcastle, Gateshead, Sunderland and South Shields, but in Fawdon and Benwell, Winlaton and Swalwell. The Radical ideals of the reformers met with little sympathy in Parliament and the protesters turned to organising mass meetings. On 16 August 1819 about 80,000 people flocked to St. Peter's Field, Manchester, to hear a speech by leading campaigner Henry Hunt, who claimed government policy was

> to get one million of the middle classes, the little shopkeepers and those people like them, to join the higher classes, in order to raise yeomanry corps and keep up standing armies, and thus united together to keep their hands still in the pockets of the seven millions.

145

The local magistrates, oblivious to the good humour of the crowd, panicked and sent the local yeomanry to arrest Hunt, but they lost control and attacked the crowd with sabres, killing eleven people. Hundreds more were injured.

No letter, diary or any other form of written record survives to indicate how those living and working on the numerous farms that comprised the Minsteracres estate fared in these desperately troubled times, but based on later testimony of the Squire as an up-to-date agriculturist and a landlord with few equals when it came to consideration of his tenants, it seems reasonable to assume that none would have suffered needlessly.

In the meantime, work continued behind the scenes to relieve England's Catholics of their additional burdens and, perhaps inevitably in this time of social tension, rumours reached Rome that the Catholic Board was having secret talks with the Prime Minster, Lord Liverpool. Cardinal Litta demanded an explanation and Dr. Poynter obtained a written assurance from Edward Jerningham, the Board's secretary that no communication of any kind had taken place between the Board and the Prime Minster, but it was to become clear later that some informal discussion had been taking place between individual Catholics and influential members of the legislature.

The question of the veto in regard to the appointment of bishops remained the principal hurdle yet to be overcome between Rome and London, but the particular point of issue on this occasion was an equally sensitive problem - the Oath of Supremacy, devised in the reign of Henry VIII in order to assert his claim to be the head of the Church of England. There were those Catholics - clergy and laity, though few in number - who believed that the Oath had been misunderstood and that it was not really inconsistent with Catholic principles. Milner, as one would expect, had always totally opposed to the Oath in any form, but his fellow bishops, according to Ward,[1] were more conciliatory, insisting that until the Government issued a statement defining the sense in which the Oath would be tendered, they were not prepared to consider it. It was common knowledge that Charles Butler wrote to Foreign Secretary Lord Grenville on 18 February 1819, expressing his personal opinion that the Oath could be rendered such that Catholics might take it, by the addition of a clause limiting the scope of the royal supremacy to such ecclesiastical matters as 'impede or prejudice' civil allegiance. Butler added, however, that most of the Catholics were not likely to accept this view unless it was recommended by the bishops, and, if asked, the bishops would have to apply to the Holy See for guidance.

A month later, we can now reveal, it was George Silvertop who was in communication with the Prime Minster, Lord Liverpool, putting forward his own comprehensive plan to 'carry the Catholic Question, not Catholic Emancipation as it is very improperly called.' In a nine-page letter, written from Lartington Hall on 20 March 20 1819, he claims to have discussed his ideas during the previous year with 'violent Orangemen and violent Catholics; with Protestant clergymen and various Dissenters' all of whom had been in general agreement about the need to reduce what Silvertop considered to be an imminent threat of violent protest in Ireland. He was therefore proposing:

> 1st. A message from the Crown requesting both Houses of Parliament to take into their consideration the laws that regulate Oaths, as now ordered to be taken in all civil and military situations, in voting for Members and Peers of Parliament and in sitting and voting in both Houses of Parliament. The great object of the message is to create a feeling in Ireland, which it would most unquestionably do, to show that their situation is near to the heart of the Sovereign and thus increase their appreciation and confidence in the British connection.

2nd. The Declaration against Transubstantiation to be entirely repealed and such Oaths ordered to be taken in all civil and military situations, and in voting for Members and Peers of Parliament, as may be judged wise, keeping the present Oath of Supremacy for University situations and those places in the Cabinet or Ireland, which it may be proper should not be filled by persons of the Roman Catholic community.

3rd. A Bill to be introduced allowing the seven Roman Catholic peers of Great Britain to assume their seats in the House of Lords and to sit and vote therein, on taking such an Oath as may be agreed upon, with power to their descendants being peers, whether Catholics or Protestant, to sit and vote therein – a clause allowing Roman Catholics in the event of the House of Peers acknowledging his having made good his title to a peerage to sit and vote therein, and the same to his descendants – a clause in the event of the Sovereign making any Roman Catholic, for his service to his country by sea or land, or in other ways, a Peer of the Realm, to sit and vote therein – a clause empowering the representative peers of Ireland, to send two Catholic peers from its number of 28 – a clause empowering the representative peers of Scotland one from its number of sixteen, that is, in each case, if the Irish or Scottish peers thought it proper to choose 2 or 1 Catholic peer to be their representative number – a clause empowering the Sovereign, in the event of any of the families of the present seven Catholic peers being extinct, to create a peer in his place, with power of voting and sitting in the House – and a clause restraining any peer having been baptised a Protestant, or having sat as a Protestant peer, from sitting and voting in the House in the event of his conforming to the Catholic religion.

4th. With respect to the House of Commons – a Bill to be introduced giving to Ireland a capacity to send 32 Members, being Roman Catholics, viz. 8 from each of the four provinces. England and Wales to have a capacity to send 16, viz. 8 from the province of Canterbury, 8 from the province of York and Scotland 2 – Each Roman Catholic at the time he takes his seat and qualifies, to sign his name in a book kept for that purpose, stating therein his being Roman Catholic – whenever the number of 32 from Ireland, 16 from England and Wales and Scotland 2 is completed, the Speaker to state the same in the ensuing London Gazette and on the vacancy occurring the same to be notified in the same manner .

5th. With respect to the ecclesiastical part of the Question, I beg leave to observe that I have always considered the Veto as neither worth asking for or refusing – for it ought to be remembered (i) that in all countries where it exists, there is a Pecuniary Establishment annexed by the Crown to the See, (ii) that the spirit of our laws and the temper of our people is very different from those on the Continent, (iii) that it has from various causes been made a most unpopular measure and the same feeling exists in Ireland with respect to it, as existed in England, among the Dissenters,[2] with respect to Lord Sidmouth's Bill, (iv) if there be two ways to obtain the same end, and that one is very hateful to a people and the other very acceptable, a wise government would not hesitate which to adopt, (v) it is presumed that if an Act were passed enacting that no person shall experience the office of Bishop in the United Empire of Great Britain and Ireland, but a native born subject thereof; that in the event of the death of any Bishop those who are in the practise of choosing his successor shall be bound to swear before one of His Majesty's Justices of the Peace, that he or they would not vote for any person to fill the vacancy but one who, to the best of their belief was a loyal, peaceable and moral man and the person so chosen should not enter upon the duties of his office, after having received his spiritual jurisdiction from the Pope, until after he had, in open court, taken the Oath of Allegiance to the King; it may be stated, I think beyond the probability of doubt, that a certainty is afforded, of obtaining loyal and peaceable persons to fill the important situation of Bishop of the Catholic Communion.[3]

It was a bold move by the Silvertop, executed one must presume, against a background of mutual respect, for during his fifteen years as Tory Prime Minister (1812-1827) Lord Liverpool was always uniformly opposed to emancipation, although not so extreme as many of his followers. Then the Catholic question, as Silvertop would call it, was always about the Irish, anyway, and it was to be upon Daniel O'Connell, rather than the King, that the fortunes of the English Catholics inevitably lay and little changed when George IV succeeded to the throne (his father, George III, died in January 1820).

Before moving on to the final years of struggle for George Silvertop and the English Catholics at large it is worth pausing to reflect on yet another well-worn Silvertop anecdote, one with nothing to do with religion or politics. It is quite apparent that the Squire, like his grandfather,[4] had an interest, if not a passion, for the arts, fostered more likely by one or both of his mentors – Henry Howard and Sir John Lawson, both of whom were grand collectors and kept extensive libraries – although it is said that when he inherited Minsteracres, it was already full of pictures and other works of art purchased by his father and grandfather during their own foreign travels.

The various sources suggest it was mainly Italian art, but first, an amusing reference to the Silvertop collection is to be found in the correspondence, previously mentioned, between the Minsteracres chaplain, Henry Rutter and his uncle, Robert Bannister. Writing in February 1788, Rutter asks his uncle for some advice regarding the Silvertop collection 'of prints and paintings, of which Mr Silvertop has a tolerable collection.'(In this instance Rutter is referring to John Silvertop, George's father). He goes on:

> Now, I know that indecent ones are neither to be looked at or kept, but I am at a loss to determine which are to be esteemed such, and whether those can be tolerated which are covered only in one part, like a crucifix, when the subject does not evidently tend to raise impure images, or those which are naked about the breast and shoulders.[5]

His uncle's reply comes directly to the point:

As to prints and paintings, their attitudes are worse than their nudities: for if they express a certain lasciviousness they will be very apt to raise the same passion in the spectator. But if there be nothing of a lascivious, wanton gesture, the nudity of the breast, shoulders, arms and legs may be tolerated: as S. Mary Magdalene in her grotto, Daniel in the den of lions, Hercules and Anteus in fight, are, I believe, represented with very little drapery. Infants are often painted quite naked, but of the male sex. The divine infant in Correggio's drawing is so, of which I have a fine engraving by Robert Strange.

As I have never seen Mr Silvertop's prints and paintings I cannot pronounce sentence upon them specifically, but if there are any Venus's, Lais's, Sappho's, or suchlike representations, he certainly ought not to expose them to the view of everyone, but to keep them concealed in his closet. And if he resents your admonitions, fear him not but show him that to occasion sins in others is a heinous scandal and he had better have a millstone tied about his neck and be cast into the sea than scandalize even one person.[6]

The prints and paintings were not mentioned again in the letters that flowed between uncle and nephew but another who had occasion to view the Squire's collection is the artist-turned-sculptor John Lough (1798-1876), the subject of another oft-quoted anecdote. Early *Memoirs* of the Silvertop family claim it was due to George Silvertop's 'help and protection that Lough became the great sculptor of whom the North is rightly proud'[7], though an examination of the facts would suggest this to be somewhat of an exaggeration. The son of a blacksmith from Muggleswick, a small village south of Minsteracres, Lough, according to his biographers, demonstrated a talent for drawing at an early age and later, with his older brother, fashioned models of gladiators in clay, which they copied from books belonging to their father.[8] As to young John's 'discovery', one story, unauthenticated, suggests a schoolmaster happened to pass the gatehouse where they lived and found young John making a clay figure, surrounded by other boys one of whom was naked and acting as a model. The master knocked at the door and reported his discovery to the young sculptor's mother, who is said to have replied in her Northumbrian dialect: 'Oh, aa'se warrant it's just our cull (simple-minded) lad making clay dollies!'

What has come to be accepted as the authenticated version, however, occurred by all accounts around 1821, and does involve George

Silvertop, who is said to have been returning home one evening from a day's foxhunting when, passing the Lough's gatehouse, he noticed legs and arms strewn all over the garden. Being curious, he dismounted and found Lough's mother in the house, who showed him her son's work lying all over the kitchen. Lough, then in his early twenties, was sent for and the Squire invited him to Minsteracres, where he is reported to have shown him works by Canova and Michaela Angelo. This much is confirmed in the diary of the artist Benjamin Haydon[9] who befriended Lough years later in London. Years later Lough is said to have told Haydon that on that first visit to Minsteracres, in his own language, 'to see Canova's works did not prick him, but Michael Angelo affected him deeply.'[10]

There seems to have been no further contact between Lough and the Squire for a while after that for, as the Rev. Lenders recalls, after serving an apprenticeship to a builder in nearby Shotley Field, young Lough left for London 'alone and friendless, and with very little money.' In an account published in 1893 accompanied by a footnote stating 'Particulars supplied to the writer by Mrs Lough' it is said that the young man from Muggleswick arrived in London in the spring of 1825 after a journey from the Tyne to the Thames, which was 'one of the most romantic episodes in his life.' He apparently 'persuaded the captain of a collier who was just sailing for London to take him on board, offering him a guinea for his passage money; but on their arrival the captain refused to take a farthing ...finally urging him not to remain in such a wilderness place as London' and offering to take him back to 'Newcassel' free of charge. Lough, however, was determined to stay in the capital and took lodgings above a grocer's shop in Burleigh Street, off The Strand. Not long afterwards the Squire heard that he was in London and called to see him but, according to the same writer, a difference of opinion led to a clash between the two.

> Silvertop wished him to go to Rome to study the models of the great Italian sculptors, and offered to defray his expenses when in Rome. Lough, however, refused to go, and said that 'he would not serve a second apprenticeship.' Mr Silvertop took offence at Lough's refusal.

Silvertop meanwhile had introduced Lough to Henry Brougham (later Lord Brougham, the Lord Chancellor) who commissioned him to produce a sculpture, and left £50 on the table. Lough, thinking nothing could be too grand for a Lord, decided upon a model of 'Milo', the Crotonian athlete.

> While Lough was thus engaged, a circumstance occurred which threatened to be the forerunner of his ruin, but which

proved, however, to be the turning point in his fortune. His room being too small for the sculpturing of 'Milo', he could not get to the upper part of the statue so as to be able to use his chisel with sufficient freedom ... With the recklessness of bold genius reduced to desperation, he actually broke through the ceiling of the room above his, and made for himself sufficient space to work at his statue. Hue and cry was instantly raised against him for this infraction of the rights of property.

The owner began to take steps for instituting legal proceedings, and even consulted Mr Brougham for this purpose. Struck with the singularity of the account, Brougham went to look at the 'Milo' and see for himself what Lough had done. On his return ...Brougham told some of his friends that he had witnessed the strangest sight that ever came before him during his whole life and narrated the circumstances. The news of the strange affair soon spread and, before long, the whole street where Lough's room was situated was lined with carriages of ladies and gentlemen, who had come to view the place and see 'Milo'.[11]

Lough was to tell later how while working on 'Milo' he did not eat meat for three months, that had only one bushel and a half of coal to warm himself through the winter, and that he used to lie down beside the damp clay model and shiver for hours until, worn out with hunger and fatigue, he fell asleep. It is also said that Brougham actually declined the statue when it was finished saying it was too big, but offered him £100 if he would go to Italy, which Lough refused.[12] However, in 1826 he had his first work accepted for the Royal Academy exhibition and later that year was admitted to the Royal Academy Schools to study sculpture[13], and soon the Press were talking of him as an 'extraordinary genius.'

However, it was the artist Haydon (who describes George Silvertop as "a friend" in his diary) together with a businessman called John Lavicount Anderdon (1792-1874) who really put Lough on the road to high-profile success by arranging his first one-man exhibition in The Great Rooms in Maddox Street, in the summer of 1827.[14] Our Squire had apparently been discussing with Haydon the idea of sending Lough to Italy for the artist, having visited Lough at his lodgings and seen the 'Milo' for himself, wrote in his diary in May of that year:

To see such a splendid effort of innate power, built up in an obscure first floor, No. 11 Burleigh St. [over] a Green Grocer's shop, without the aid of education, Foreign travel, Patronage, money, or even food, is only another instance of the innate vigour & natural power which no aid or instruction can supply the want of. If he goes to Italy he will be ruined! What becomes of all those who go & doze in the Vatican? They come back castrated! Lough, [un] like Chantrey, did not put off his hour or inspiration till he was independent. Alas, he could not. His genius sat on him night and day like an Incubus – goaded, haunted, pressed, worried, drove him to exertion ...Lough will be a great man. He has all the consciousness of Genius, with great modesty. The only fear is, he is so soon ripe, & has so mature a style, that he may, if not perpetually curbed by nature, get into manner ...the more I reflect on this extraordinary work, the more delighted I am.

Lough's one-man exhibition followed a month later (June, 1827) but it was an incident that occurred at the private view, attended by Silvertop, prior to the public opening, that Haydon describes in his diary:

The Duke of Wellington entered ...I never saw one whose air & presence were so unlike genius or heroism. He seemed embarrassed, and as if he felt he was unpopular. The Duke felt great admiration indeed, and going to the books opened,

160

wrote with his own illustrious right hand, which had by its pointing and as the means of conveying the conceptions of his great Genius, destroyed Napoleon! – an order for Milo & Samson. It was done in a spirited manner. He then turned round. One of Lough's Patrons[15] came over and shook his Grace by the hand and thanked him. The Duke turned round and said, 'He should go abroad', in his loud, distinct and military voice. Silvertop, who had just heard my opinion, hesitated. The Duke of Wellington, surprised at not being acceded to, half blushed, & said, 'Not to stay, but to see, eh, the, eh, great works, eh, that others have done'. He then turned round. I bowed to thank him, & he walked out. He touched his hat, like a military man, to me & to all.

According to the Dictionary of British Sculptors[16] Lough, whose works adorned the top of the grand staircase at Minsteracres in days gone by (see illustration), did eventually go to Italy, studying there between 1835-39, but there is no evidence to suggest that George Silvertop had anything to do with his decision, other than perhaps putting the idea in his head in the first place.

Now, returning to the serious business at hand, it is necessary to bring the reader up to date on what had been happening in Ireland for it was they who took the upper hand in the early 1820s with the foundation of the Catholic Association. It was Daniel O'Connell's idea and his objectives were two fold: to re-unite the Irish Catholic body by healing the breach caused by the Veto question and, secondly, to inspire the people with enthusiasm and make them aware of the power they collectively possessed. For he had made up his mind that victory had to be won by the people themselves, not by the upper classes alone.[17] Initial meetings of the Association were so poorly attended that difficulty was often found in making up the modest quorum of ten, as required by the rules before a meeting could be attended. Then O'Connell introduced his masterstroke: in addition to the 'members' who subscribed £1 2s 9d a year, he proposed there should be 'associates' who would pay only one shilling a year. It was a clever way of inviting the whole body of Irish Catholics - i.e., the vast majority of the population - to join, calling the levy by the curious name the 'Catholic Rent'. It did the trick – by the end of the first year (1823) over £1,000 a week 'rent' was flowing in and it was not long before the English Catholics recognised its potential and decided to follow suit. The old (English) Catholic Board, after all, had been strictly limited to the aristocracy and landed gentry and, like the Irish, there was a genuine desire to get more people involved, including ecclesiastics and, according to Ward, the founding of the Association marked the beginning of a new relationship between the English laity and its clergy and bishops.[18]

There was nothing analogous to the 'Catholic Rent', which in view of the small number of English Catholics would have been totally impracticable, but in order to raise extra funds, a general subscription of £1 a year was introduced. There was to be a committee consisting of the four vicars-apostolic and all the Catholic noblemen *ex officio,* together with fifty elected members, and the first meeting was held at the Freemason's Tavern in London on 2 June 1823, the Duke of Norfolk presiding. Silvertop and all his closest friends, Charles Butler, John Lingard, Henry Howard and Henry Lawson, along with most other members of the old Catholic Board, simply transferred their allegiance *en bloc* to the new Association and, in addition, local Associations were established in major Catholic centres, such as Newcastle. In practical terms little was accomplished in England by the change of name – apart from perhaps attracting new members, though they were not in the same number as the Irish – but there were two distinct advantages to the new Association(s). Firstly, as already stated, there evolved between the laity and clergy in England a new respect for each other's points of view, but more importantly, there was, for the moment at least, a greater degree of co-operation between the English and Irish Catholic bodies, which had the effect of giving O'Connell much increased status.

A descendant of an old Catholic family, O'Connell had benefited from the Relief Act of 1793 by being called to the Irish bar in 1798. Discovering a talent for popular oratory, he became its leading figure in less than ten years and now at this time, when the older Catholic movement, the movement of Parliamentarians, was rotting in stagnation, O'Connell emerged in full stature. Consequently it was he who now took the lead - on behalf of Catholics on both sides of the water - and completed the course to emancipation in triumph, for the good of all.

References & Notes:

[1] Ward – Eve, vol. ii, p. 253.

[2] Numerous among the middle and working classes, Dissenters were the Protestants outside the established Church of England, including the Presbyterians, Baptists, Quakers and others. Their grievance stemmed from the fact that they were denied full civil rights yet like everyone else, were taxed to support the Established Church.

[3] British Library, Add. MSS 38276.31

[4] According to Welford's *Men of Mark twixt Tyne & Tweed*, George Silvertop senior was an early patron of Thomas Bewick, the engraver, p. 395.

[5] Gooch, p. 121.

[6] *Ibid*, p. 123.

[7] Lenders, p. 112.

[8] John Lough & Elizabeth Merson (nee Lough), *John Graham Lough*, The Boydell Press, 1987, p. 3 (hereafter Lough).

[9] William Bissell Pope, *The Diary of Benjamin Robert Haydon*, Harvard University Press, *1963*, (hereafter, Pope).

[10] *Ibid*, p. 4.

[11] G.Neasham, *North Country Sketches, Notes, Essays and Reviews*, Durham, 1983, pp.9-11.

[12] *Ibid*.

[13] Lough, p. 8.

[14] Pope, p. 198.

[15] Haydon may of course have been referring to George Silvertop, but it is more likely to have been Lord Egremont (1751-1837), patron of Turner and other artists, who admired Lough's work, Charles Cockerell (1788-1863), an architect and classical archaeologist, who with William Bigg (1755-1828) arranged the Rooms for the exhibition, or Anderdon (*qv*) who helped Haydon organise it.

[16] Rupert Gunnis, *Dictionary of British Sculptors*, The Abbey Library, London, p. 243. Lough died in 1876 and, according to the Dictionary, his obituary in the *Art Journal* declared, 'in private life no artist has been more largely esteemed and respected. His personal friends were numerous, including many of the most famous men and women of the age in science, art and letters.'

[17] Ward-Eve, vol. iii, p. 112.

[18] *Ibid*, vol. iii, p. 116.

Chapter Ten

A moment in history

Before moving on to the reign of George 1V this is perhaps the moment to reintroduce the young boy who had been drawn to a window in Durham by a rowdy mob of anti-Catholic protestors back in 1807. Nicholas Wiseman was eight when he entered Ushaw College, just two years before Silvertop's friend John Lingard, then vice-President, left to pursue his literary career. It seems that Lingard must have sensed a latent ability in the quiet, retiring child for he is said to have given him encouragement and kind attention. According to Wiseman's biographer, the young student was 'grateful for these specific acts of thoughtful and delicate kindness, which showed a tender heart' and he was to remember them many years later when he wrote that though Lingard 'went from college soon after, and I later left the country and saw him not again for fifteen years, yet there grew up an understanding first, and by degrees a correspondence and an intimacy between us, which continued to the close of his life.'[1] It is said that shortly after his birth Wiseman's mother laid him on the altar of the Cathedral of Seville and dedicated him to the service of the Church. His biographer, however, suggests that it was while he was at Ushaw that Wiseman finally determined to enter the priesthood. He tells the story of Wiseman being forced to take shelter from a thunder storm in a cottage, and that while for half an hour the storm raged, his mind, always susceptible to romantic impressions, was made up by the thunder and lightning as to his life's vocation.[2]

By the time he came to leave Ushaw, in October 1818, at the age of sixteen, Wiseman had proved himself to be an exceptional student, and was chosen as one of the first ten – five from the North, four from London and one from the West - to enter the recently reopened English College in Rome, his home for the next twenty-two years. The *Venerabile Collegio Inglese* had originally been a *hospitium* for English pilgrims to the tomb of the Apostle, and as such could trace its descent to Saxon times. After the breach with Rome the house first became a place of refuge for English Catholic priests until in 1578 it was converted into a college by Pope Gregory XIII, and so it remained until 1798 when the English College, along with many other ancient institutions in Rome, was plundered by the French revolutionary armies. For the next twenty years the college remained derelict and empty until, at the suggestion of Cardinal Consalvi, the aged Pius VII, Napoleon's former prisoner, whose long and eventful reign was nearing its end, decided to reopen it.

The journey to Rome undertaken by Wiseman and his fellow students in the winter of that year is worth recalling, if only as an example of the hazards faced by travellers in the early nineteenth century. They had chosen to travel by sea under sail from Liverpool to Leghorn (northern Italy); embarking on 2 October, and in a letter to his mother the following April, Wiseman wrote:

> Saturday the 18 of October was the most fatal day or our voyage. It was rough weather all day and towards 10 at night the wind became more favourable but the sea still remained very high. On a sudden we were alarmed with a cry: 'All hands on deck!' We all ran up and found that a man had just fallen overboard. It was truly awful to hear the cries of the poor man in the water. Ropes and spars were thrown over to no purpose, and our captain with another sailor went out in a boat, with danger of their lives, but was too late. The man lost was a black and our best sailor. We tossed about the ocean for some days longer, till on the eve of All Saints we saw Lisbon Rock after having been 22 days without seeing land.

At another point the ship caught fire and it seems accidents were not confined to human beings for Wiseman wrote that later, in the Mediterranean, 'A dog which we had on board went mad and after howling around the deck and refusing

168

water, went to the stern and jumped overboard.'[3] Even the journey by road across Italy had its moments, for the bodies of executed highwaymen were apparently suspended from poles along the road outside Florence. Finally in Rome, Wiseman described their grim welcome in the 'wide and lofty corridors' of their new home, the whole house bearing evidence of not having been inhabited for nearly a generation. The old church of the Holy Trinity, which had formed part of the ancient hospice, was still standing, but the roof was gone, all the altars had been removed, and the various tombs and monuments had been desecrated. Wiseman wrote that the students

> wandered through the solemn building and made it, after years of silence, re-echo to the sound of English voices, and give back the bounding tread of those who had returned to claim their own.[4]

In the unfortunate absence of Henry Howard's diaries, there is no evidence to suggest that he and George Silvertop met Wiseman or any of the other students when they visited Rome in 1820 on their 'Milner Mission' but the re-opening of the college was of such significance it is reasonable to assume that they would have paid a visit and met the students. It is not too fanciful either to suppose that the Silvertop might also have met another young Englishman who

169

happened to be visiting Italy at this particular moment. His name was George Spencer, the youngest of seven children of a prominent Protestant aristocratic English family, whose eventual conversion to Catholicism would be noted in England among 'the first fruits of Emancipation.'[5] He too was destined in the years ahead to enter the celebrated portals of the English College as a student, an event with little particular relevance to our story at present, but which was to set in train a whole sequence of events that, over a century later, would directly concern the Silvertops of Minsteracres. More of that later, however, for in the meantime it needs explaining that Spencer, born in 1799, was the son of the second Earl Spencer of Althorp, who had been First Lord of the Admiralty during the Napoleonic Wars. The eldest son had been a Member of Parliament for a number of years and would eventually become Chancellor of the Exchequer (1830), but it was a familiar custom at the time that the youngest of the family be directed towards talking Holy Orders and so George spent some years at Eton before entering Trinity College, Cambridge, where by a perfunctory attendance at the divinity classes, he obtained his degree with a certificate which admitted him to ordination whenever he felt so inclined.[6]

First though, at the age of twenty, he set off with his parents on a Grand Tour, which lasted the whole of 1820. Taking their own four carriages[7] they travelled on the Continent, from Paris to Milan to Rome to Sicily and homewards through Austria and Germany. His biographer records that it was at the Paris Opera that the troublesome chords of Mozart's *Don Giovanni* called him to repentance[8], while another of his biographers reveals Spencer's own account of the event:

> The most remarkable impression of religion which I remember in all this period, was in a place where it might have been least expected ... I went to see the opera of Don Giovanni ... the last scene of it represents Don Giovanni, the hero of the piece, seized in the midst of his licentious career by a troop of devils, and hurried down to hell. As I saw this scene, I was terrified at my own state. I knew that God, who knew what was within me, must look on me as one in the same class with such as Don Giovanni, and for once this holy fear of God's judgement saved me: and this holy warning I was to find in an opera house at Paris.[9]

His biographer says, however, that while in Rome his first thoughts were of St. Peter's, the Catholic Church remained, at the end of the tour, what it was to him at the beginning – a symbol for 'priests, processions, incense and mummery.'[10] Back home, in 1823, he was installed as curate in charge of the Protestant parish of Great Brington, comprising a group of villages close to the family seat at Althorp, and received 'priest's orders' the following year. There we shall leave the young Spencer, to return later, but in the meantime, this was a particularly stressful period for George Silvertop, for when he himself returned from the Continent it was to find that his brother Henry was in serious financial difficulties.

Fate had on the one hand been particularly unkind to Henry Thomas Silvertop. Five years younger than George – the brother in between, John, died aged twenty – he was therefore not entitled to any part of the Silvertop landed estates, and he even had to forego the £6,000 bequeathed him by his father because of those debts. On the other hand, when he eventually came to leave home, it could be said his prospects were far superior to those of older brother George, for not only did he marry well, but he was also to benefit enormously from being his mother's favourite. There is nothing to indicate whether Henry pursued any kind of career after completing his education at Crook Hall, Durham (the predecessor to Ushaw College) but his great nephew, the Rev. George Silvertop, describes him in his *Memoirs* as 'an ardent geologist ... He was an F.G.S., F.R.S. etc., and author of a work called *Observations on Fossil Vegetables*, published 1831'. In any case, he was just twenty one years of age when in 1800 he married Eliza Witham[11], daughter of Thomas Witham of Headlam who, more importantly, was the chosen heiress of her wealthy uncle William Witham[12], of Cliffe, on the Durham/Yorkshire border, who died just two years later. Henry promptly changed his name by Royal licence to Witham and joined (*jure uxoris*) the landed gentry class as Squire of the Cliffe estate, though in time, through his mother, he was to assume even greater status. In the meantime, Henry Silvertop Witham and his wife Eliza produced ten children, six sons and four daughters; their first child, Catherine, born in 1801, who was destined to secure her own special place in the story of the Silvertops[13], they named after Henry's mother.

Probably due to the cash limitations imposed by her husband's expansive building programme, the older Mrs Silvertop had been obliged to remain on in her widowhood as mistress of Minsteracres Hall under the patronage of her eldest son George, but her circumstances were about to take a dramatic turn for the better. An uncle, John Maire, of Gray's Inn, had left three valuable estates – Lartington, near Barnard Castle, Hutton Henry, south of Durham, and Hardwicke, on the Durham coast – to Mrs Silvertop's brother, Henry Lawson, for the elder brother, Sir Henry Lawson, already controlled the family's Brough estate. Maire's will added the proviso, however, that should the eldest brother die without heir, and Henry succeed to the title and Brough estate, the Maire estates

173

should go to the sister, Catherine. And that is in fact exactly what happened: in 1811 the Matriach of Minsteracres became the owner of Lartington, Hardwick and Hutton Henry and immediately began calling herself Mrs Silvertop Maire. The good news for favourite son Henry was that his mother was quite happy living at Minsteracres – her home for the past forty years and, after all, son George was more often in London than at home – and as a result she suggested that Henry and his large family should move into Lartington Hall. Moreover, she gave him complete control over her affairs so that he effectively became Squire of four estates.[14] Regrettably, Henry Silvertop Witham seemed to have inherited his father's lack of finesse in financial matters, prompting one of his sons to remark rather caustically after his death: 'If it had not been for my father's extravagance, I would have been the richest commoner in England!'[15] There exists no detailed account of how Henry came to get into such a mess but another relative spelt out a contributing factor to his problems:

That Harry (Henry) Witham did not keep racehorses seems not to have prevented him from losing large sums on the turf. I have heard from a person who was living at the time, that a great dance or ball was prepared by him at Lartington to celebrate the event of 'Doctor Syntax' winning for him a large sum, which was to re-establish his shattered fortunes. In the midst of this, news arrived that 'Doctor Syntax'[16] had lost the race. The ball was abandoned and Harry Witham made a bolt for John o'Groats to escape from his creditors.[17]

Much local money had been wagered on the 'Catholic Horse', as it was known, and Henry's already massive debts meant that he had no option but to make a dramatic flight to Scotland in 1821, leaving elder brother George to step in to try and save the family name, though once again we have no record of exactly how he managed to bring matters under control. That he was not entirely successful in sparing the Silvertop name is evidenced by the fact that the Rev. George Silvertop claims in his *Memoirs* to have read the original of a letter, written in May 1823 by a Canon Thomas Slater, the priest in charge of the Mission at Hutton Henry. Addressed to George Silvertop at Minsteracres, it read:

> Honrd. Sir, No consideration less than the destitute condition to which the Catholic congregation of Hardwick will be reduced in the event of the property passing out of the hands of its present most worthy possessor could have induced me to intrude upon your attention. But as the event seems next to certain that Lord D(arlington) will become the purchaser, the only remaining hope I have is to

propose to your consideration the separating some detached spot (say, for example 2 or ? acres adjoining the road to the Hutton Henry estate) which if it met with your approval I would purchase and erect a chapel thereon. The only apology I have to make in thus presuming is the urgent solicitude of this congregation not to be left without some place of worship, and the desire I have not to have to witness such a scene.

There is no possibility of obtaining one foot of land near here for the purpose were I even disposed to do so, and the only hope is in your hands of a chapel being continued or lost for ever. I am well aware that they may be many insurmountable difficulties to my proposal did it even meet with your approval, but of course being totally ignorant of your arrangements I can only leave it in its most simple form a bare proposition. (At the same time most humbly pressing it upon your consideration.) My hopes of ever having an offer of Hardwick, which you so kindly intimated, were blighted when I saw Ld. D's surveyor enter the premises. –Excuse the great liberty I have taken in addressing you and attribute it entirely to the earnest desire that I feel of not seeing the poor people deserted and permit me with the greatest respect to subscribe myself.

It appears from what follows that no notice was taken of this letter but the Rev. Silvertop suggests it might never have been delivered to Minsteracres, for the original he saw had the following comments added, in the same handwriting but with a different pen, on a blank page in the letter:

The Mission had been at Hardwick from time immemorial and Harry Witham's extravagances forced him to sell it to Lord Darlington. George Silvertop, Harry's brother had the management. No provision was made to continue the Mission and if I had not come forward with my private means, this Mission had been lost. This was the letter I wrote to George Silvertop Esq., the brother of Harry Witham to whom Hardwick belonged and who had the management of his estates on sale. Hy. Witham and Silvertop did nothing. Ld. Darlington sold me the moiety for the same price he gave for it 11 acres more or less. Thus proving that Harry Witham and George Silvertop had less feeling than the heretic Ld. Darlington, who always and after when (*sic* Ld.) Cleveland showed his goodness to me in the Hartlepool Chapel. Give me such as

Ld. Cleveland before 10,000 of your H. Withams and Geo. Silvertops although they professed themselves Catholics and the Duke was what was called a Heretic.

'P.S. What a fool I was for inditing such a letter to Silvertop!!!!! As above.[18]

Henry's debts, meanwhile, must have been significant for three of the four estates – Cliffe, Hardwick and Hutton Henry – had to be sold before he could safely be summoned home from across the border. None of the estates, of course, had actually belonged to him (Cliffe was his wife's property; the other two belonged to his mother) leaving just Lartington Hall (which also belonged to his mother) where he lived out the rest of his days. Henry clearly managed to redeem himself in later years for in 1932 her was appointed High Sheriff of County Durham and after his death a Witham Testimonial building was erected in Barnard's Castle, entirely by public donations, in his memory.[19] For big brother George, nonetheless, it was a long and wearisome process; just how long is evidenced by a letter he wrote to his friend John Lingard in December 1826, in which he announced: 'I am happy to tell you that I am near closing my brother Witham's most troublesome Trust, which will be an immense weight off my shoulders.'[20] Unfortunately for George, dark clouds of a very different kind had already gathered on the horizon as a result of a speech he had made that summer (April 1826). The occasion was a special dinner in the Assembly Rooms in Newcastle in honour of Viscount Howick, son and heir of Earl Grey, who had just been elected to represent his father's old Northumberian parliamentary constituency. Called upon to address the gathering, Silvertop said that as one who had 'felt the chilling powers of laws of exclusion and witnessed their withering effects on others' he wished to express his joy at the way in which his audience had responded to the toast 'The cause of civil and religious liberty all over the world.' He went on:

> Maintaining, as I have always done, that liberty and conscience is the alienable right of all men, hating and detesting persecution, whether enforced by Catholic despots or Protestant states; whether effected by blood, by inquisition or by deprivation of honours, office or franchise, I hail, Sir, the cheering manner in which this toast has been received, as another proof of that animating principle, the spread of civil and religious freedom throughout the world.

Warming to his theme, the Squire said he was compelled to speak on some serious issues.

> It is stated that Catholics are intolerant because they maintain for themselves

exclusive salvation. Perhaps, Sir, the best way to reply to this statement will be by personal argument. I see near me a learned friend of mine who is descended of Catholic parents, was baptized in the Catholic church, was educated in Catholic principles, and who, after most mature consideration has completely satisfied his mind of the truth, and has espoused the principles of the reformed church. I, sir, like him, am descended from Catholic parents, was baptized by a Catholic clergyman, have been educated in Catholic principles, and have after many an hour's thought, satisfied my mind of the truths of the pure principles of faith of the Romish Church, in the discipline of which, I most sincerely and anxiously wish to a complete and radical reform. Now, Sir, do I believe that the gates of Heaven are closed on my learned friend, because in the sincerity of his conviction he has expressed the principles of the reformed church? God forbid I should entertain any such opinion, God forbid I should be guilty of what appears to me would be a blasphemy towards my Creator, who in his kindness towards man, has endowed him with the gift of reason. In the exercise of that great blessing, we have arrived at different conclusions; and although we have so done, I entertain not a particle of doubt,

180

but that with good works, the gates of Heaven will be open to us both.

The Squire defended his involvement with the British and Foreign Bible Society, which he described as 'one of the greatest efforts of the piety and sincerity of man', and referred to a letter written by the late Pontiff, Pius VII – 'that most excellent man' – to the Bishops of Great Britain, urging them 'to encourage the reading of the Holy Scriptures among the Catholics under their spiritual care, as the best antidotes against the infidel and immoral publications of the day.' He then recalled the meeting he had organised in Newcastle back in 1815 to protest against the persecution of Protestants in France and said that some time later he had, while travelling on the Continent, visited all those places (Nismes, Montpellier, Bordeaux etc.) where the most respectable Protestants in France lived. The promise he made to them was to return their thanks to every Englishman who took a part in their relief, and he was now performing that promise. Concluding his speech, which according to the newspaper report was accompanied by much cheering and applause, Silvertop criticised recent declarations by some Irish orators, who, he said, had harmed the Catholic cause, but he expressed the hope that the time had now come, or was near at hand, when every man, in every clime, would be allowed to adore his God according to the dictates of his own conscience, without fear or punishment, or the deprivation of honour or civil office, or franchise.[21]

Whether or not the Squire of Minsteracres was conscious of the storm his words would evoke from the ultra orthodox Catholics among the English body, we shall never know, but it is indeed ironic that it was barely a fortnight after that speech in Newcastle that the news came of the death of Dr. Milner, in response to which the *Truthteller*[22] exclaimed:

> O weep, ye Friends of Religion, for the loss of her unbending and invincible Champion! Mourn, ye Lovers of Truth of her most undaunted and indefatigable Defender! Milner! Whose name has resounded through the four quarters of the globe, and is venerated by every admirer of public integrity, genuine piety, and brilliant talent – Milner, the Athanasius of the nineteenth century – is numbered among the dead!

References & Notes:

[1] Ward - Eve, vol. 1, p. 8.

[2] Brian Fothergill, *Nicholas Wiseman,* Faber & Faber, 1963, p. 20 (hereafter, Fothergill).

[3] English College Archives, *Venerabile,* vol. IV, no. 2, April 1929.

[4] Cardinal Wiseman, *Recollections of the last four Popes,* 1856, p. 7.

[5] Ward – Eve, vol. 3, p. 281.

[6] Denis Gwynn, *The Second Spring 1818-52,* Burns Oates, 1942, p. 27.

[7] *The Spencer Diaries,* Minsteracres Archives.

[8] Fothergill, p. 58.

[9] Father Pius, *Life of Father Ignatius of St. Paul,* 1866, p. 90.

[10] Urban Young, *Life of Father Ignatius Spencer,* London, 1933, p. 14 (hereafter, Young)

[11] It was this marriage that, as we shall see later, provided the continuation of the Silvertop line after the death of older brother George.

[12] William Witham was the grandfather of Henry Howard, of Corby Castle, George Silvertop's mentor.

[13] Catherine married Henry Englefield in 1824 and their first born, Henry Charles was destined to become George Silvertop's heir.

[14] Silvertop, p. 15.

[15] Edward Thomas Witham (later R.R. Monsignor) quoted by Silvertop, p.19.

[16] Dr. Syntax, a famous thoroughbred racehorse owned by Ralph Riddel, and winner of 20 Gold Cups, was named after a popular fictional nineteenth century clergyman and had at least two public houses in Northumberland named after him.

[17] Silvertop, p. 19.

[18] *Ibid,* pp. 16-17.

[19] Alan Wilkinson, *Barnard Castle, Historic Market Town,* Smith Settle, 1998.

[20] Cambridge University Library, Add. MSS 9418/15/63.

[21] *Newcastle Weekly Chronicle,* April 15, 1826.

[22] The *Truthseller* was the latest publishing venture of William Eusebius Andrews, former editor/proprietor of the *Orthodox Journal* which ceased publication in 1820. In the interim Andrews had started three other publications – *The Catholic Vindicator, The Catholic Advocate of Civil and Religious Liberty* and *The Advocate,* but all had failed. The *Truthseeker* was established as a weekly newspaper in September 1824 but lasted only twelve months, after which it continued as a pamphlet until 1829 when it too was finally discontinued.

George Silvertop
As portrayed by Richard Welford in his publication *Men of Mark Twixt Tyne and Tweed* published in 1895

Chapter Eleven

A surprise attack

Dissension within the ranks during the struggle for emancipation was by all accounts not a phenomenon limited to the comparatively small, top-heavy body of Catholics in England; the very much larger Irish community had its own problems, too, particularly on the question of the Veto, but there was a marked difference between the two bodies, as the Milner affair adequately demonstrated – and George Silvertop was about to discover - in that, in England, it all got very personal.

Milner, of course, always argued that he acted with the highest moral principles when promoting the bitter confrontations that became such a feature of his life, although let us not forget that the Rev. Bramston once said of him that he was 'the author of more mischief against the Church than Luther himself.'[1] No one else among the ecclesiastical English Catholics seemed prepared to speak publicly of him in such terms, but there must have been more than a few – both clerical and lay - who would have hoped that the divisions he created would begin to heal upon his demise. This, it seems, was not to be, at least not while the likes of William Eusebius Andrews were ready, willing and able to take up his mantle.

[Much like the tabloid proprietors of the current day, it would not have escaped Andrews' notice that scandal and controversy are the foundation of profit in the publishing business; if it did, it was a lesson he learned to his cost when Dr. Milner stopped writing for his previous publication, the *Orthodox Journal,* causing its demise. Now, without questioning his genuine beliefs, it seems that with his latest publication, *The Truthteller,* already faltering through lack of support, Andrews set out to create the controversy himself.]

Thus, barely a week after the Newcastle meeting addressed by Silvertop, *The Truthteller, No.* 28, carried a twelve-page article written by Andrews himself, which began on the front page with the heading: ' TO THE CATHOLICS OF THE UNITED KINGDOM' and opened: 'My Friends and Fellow Sufferers ...' Telling his readers that he had originally prepared an address to the Protestants of England, he said he had been thwarted in his intentions 'by the officious intrusion of Mr George Silvertop's sentiments at Newcastle-upon-Tyne, which have found their way into the old *Times* and other London prints, as well as the three Newcastle papers, and therefore have been pretty profusely circulated, to the very great detriment of your cause.' But before launching into a point-by-point denunciation of the Squire's Newcastle speech, Andrews spelled out his 'Milnerian' credentials:

> I have frequently had occasion to address you on the peculiarity of your situation, but I do not recollect to have done so under more painful feelings than the present. For thirteen years I have advocated your cause against the attacks of your bigoted foes, and it has occasionally imposed upon me as a duty to expose the insidious conduct of men who profess to be your friends. This latter obligation, I assure you, has been and is now the most irksome task I have to perform; nevertheless, as the friend and defender of Truth, I should fail in my duty were I now to shrink from detecting the sly designs of the latter, when openly and unblushingly made, any more than the falsehoods of the former. I have said that your situation is peculiar, and certainly, when you have not only to sustain the undivided and unceasing attacks of hundreds of sectarians, but have also to

defend the inerrability of your religious principles from the misrepresentations of the ignorant or treacherous of your own body, it must be conceded that your case is a singular one, and requires the utmost circumspection to keep it in its proper light before the public eye.

Urging his readers to embrace consistency and integrity, 'that you may be a guide to public opinion, in the midst of the vacillating notions of our would-be-thought superendowed fellow subjects', Andrews finally got to the point:

These observations, my friends, are addressed to you in consequence of what has passed, and is passing, in the sister island relative to the question of emancipation, and what has taken place at a dinner given last week to Lord Howick, at Newcastle-upon-Tyne, on occasion of his canvassing for the representation of the County of Northumberland in Parliament ....There were several Catholic gentlemen present who, I understand, were extremely disgusted with the speech of Mr Silvertop, and it was listened to generally with much impatience and disapprobation. I am informed that the reports given of this speech are very defective, and must have undergone some revision, as it was, my informant says, by far more reprehensible than it appears in print.

Andrews began his denunciation in a conciliatory manner, saying he agreed with Silvertop that the speeches by the Irish leaders 'after suffering themselves to be cheated of their political independence and consistency in England' had been anything but satisfactory, but the tone ended there:

> but while Mr. Silvertop was censuring the Irish orators for their want of sagacity and prudence, he ought to have kept a bridle on his own tongue, and saved himself the disgrace of being either an ignorant or a trickish advocate of the cause he volunteered to defend. I unite with Mr. S. in maintaining "that liberty of conscience is the inalienable right of all men" and "hating and detesting *persecution*, whether enforced by Catholic despots or Protestant States", but I am not disposed to go as far as to acknowledge with him, that Catholics have persecuted Protestants as *Protestants*, though it cannot be denied that Protestants have persecuted Catholics, for no other cause than their adherence to the right of conscience. From my view of history it is clear to me that persecution would not have been known, if the children of error had confined themselves to the same

weapons to propagate their notions which the Catholic missionaries employed in overcoming error – namely, argument and persuasion.

But this method was not adapted to convince those who were in possession of truth to forsake it, and therefore violent means were resorted to, which compelled the Catholic monarchs and states to seek the security of property and order by strong measures, calculated to restrain the lawless depredations of innovation. These were certainly the motives that gave rise to the laws against the Lollards, which were not enacted until the nation had been thrown into confusion by the risings of the ignorant people who had been infected with the then dangerous novelties of the day. But this was not the case with the laws passed against Catholics in the reigns of Henry VII, Edward VI, Elizabeth, and the Stuarts. The Statute Book bears evidence that the prevention of the growth of Popery was aimed at by our penal law makers; that it was conscience, and conscience only, the Catholics were persecuted for; every act that was passed, during the long period named, aimed at the extirpation of the Catholic *religion*, not of the physical resistance of its professors to lawful authority; which religion a powerful; writer has invincibly proved was the greatest blessing to the people of this country ever felt by them. It is therefore plainly manifest, that the best way to advance the cause of emancipation is to undeceive the people, and not to cater to the appetites of the prejudiced, by admitting that which is not exactly true.

Andrews then turned to Silvertop's reference to 'exclusive salvation', dismissing it as having been 'totally misrepresented'. He said that if the Squire was sincere in his statements 'he is no more a Catholic than is Dr. Fenwick.' We cannot be certain that Silvertop actually used the man's name in his Newcastle speech, but Dr. Fenwick is presumably the man he was reported as referring to as 'a friend.' In any case, Andrews went on:

> The introduction of this gentleman's name was most indelicate and reprehensible. It was a public exposition entirely uncalled for; and had I been Dr. Fenwick I would have given Mr. Silvertop such a rap over the knuckles for his personal allusion, as should have made them tingle whilst he lived. Mr. Silvertop commenced his speech by saying he was one of those persons who still remain attached to the *pure principles* of the *ancient faith;* but if he really believes that Dr. Fenwick stands as good a chance for Heaven, after *abandoning* the *pure*

principles of the *ancient faith,* as he who still adheres to them, he must be put down by every man of common sense as a stark mad fool.

The insults did not end there. Declaring that he (Andrews) did not mean that all Protestants were doomed to eternal damnation – 'God forbid that such a thought should be entertained by any Catholic' – he continued:

Of the chance between Mr. Silvertop and Dr. Fenwick for the gates of Heaven, there *may* be very little difference; I hope that both will have the good fortune to enter them; and were I authorized to give an opinion, I should think that Dr. Fenwick stands the best chance; for Mr. Silvertop says the doctor left the Catholic church for the *reformed* one "in the *sincerity* of his conviction", whereas Mr. S. makes a ridiculous profession of adhering to a *pure* church; in which he "most sincerely and most anxiously wish to see a complete and RADICAL reform." The reports have got it a reform in the *discipline* of the Church; I am, however, assured, my friends, by persons that were present, that the eloquent orator was not so mealy-mouthed, but expressed his wish for a *reform,* nay, a *radical reform in the Church,*

191

and yet professed to believe in *its pure principles!!!*

Suggesting that Silvertop should perhaps follow Dr. Fenwick's example by joining the reformed church – 'would it not be better for the Church cause that such men should cease to take a lead in your affairs?'- Andrews continued by pouring scorn on the Squire's membership of the Bible Society:

Here, my friends, is the great evil you have laboured under in your wishes and endeavours to rescue yourselves from a state of civil proscription and unmerited calumny. Those who should stoutly contest for the honour of our creed inch by inch, until a thorough conviction is wrought in the public mind in favour of Catholicism, endeavour, by false steps and parasitical conduct, to sooth those prejudices which can never be radically cured but by firmness of principle, combined with true freedom; not that sickening show of false liberality, so common in these days of refinement, which flatters a man in his errors, provided he will grant his assistance to further your temporal views. But what can we expect from a person who professes to be a Catholic, and yet has the effrontery to boast of his being a member, nay, an officer of the British and Foreign Bible Society, and of having contributed to its funds, though it is well known that the object of this society is opposed to the interests of true religion.

Mr. Silvertop, a professed Catholic, considers this institution 'one of the greatest efforts of the *piety* and SINCERITY of man', although he cannot be ignorant that its object is to proselytise the Catholic from his church, and one of the reports makes him acknowledge that he was acquainted with instances of this nature, which he said "shed an *unpopularity* on its *real* principles." We sincerely wish Mr. Silvertop would confine himself in future to *political* topics, and not venture again in the sphere beyond the comprehension of his mind. He is either most profoundly ignorant of the doctrines of his own church, and the real principles of the far-famed institution of which he is an officer and contributor, or he is what I will not state upon paper. At all events he is a *false* doctor of Catholic theology, and therefore it becomes you to disown him.'

There were more insults to follow, in reference to the meeting of Catholics in Newcastle back in 1815, only on this occasion Andrews was able to draw support from the venerable Dr. Milner.

Describing Silvertop's speech on that occasion as 'an oration made as famous for its false premises and bad theology as his present harangue', Andrews went on:

> I was the first to oppose the logic and doctrine of this Gentleman on that occasion, and I had the happiness to have the concurrence of the venerable and venerated Dr. Milner, who likewise condemned the proposition set forth by this meeting, of which Mr. Silvertop was the chairman. The improper proceedings at that meeting had been exploded, not only as they regarded the doctrine of the Catholic Church, but also the invidious cry of *Persecution* so unjustly raised at that time against the Bourbon Government of France by the bigots of this country. Why then he should refer to this period I am not able to divine, unless it was to indulge somewhat in personal vanity, by letting the company know he had been a great traveller, though it would seem without any improvement. But Mr. Silvertop made a *promise*, it appears, to the Protestants of France, that he would return thanks to every Englishman who took part in their relief; that is, to those busy ill-natured zealots who raised the cry of *"No Popery"* and *"Persecution"*, and the credulous gulls who echoed the cry without knowing its

meaning; and he takes the opportunity of an electioneering dinner to fulfil this promise and defame his brethren in faith!!! Well, may we, my friends, exclaim, Oh! Save us from our friends, when we have such advocates and expounders of our principles as Mr. George Silvertop.

With a final call to his 'friends and fellow sufferers' to 'put to shame' characters 'who disgrace so respectable a body as you form, headed by the most ancient and virtuous aristocracy in the kingdom', Andrews concluded:

> Catholics of England and Ireland! Have I not shown you that your interests are as much, if not more, injured by the injudicious and unwarrantable conduct of vain and ambitious men in your own body, as by the calumnious attacks of the bigots and hirelings amongst the Protestants? Come forward, then, and disavow the mischievous policy of temporising measures; disown these would-be leaders who mistake your faith, and disguise your principles, to deceive those whom you ought to convince.[2]

We have no evidence to suggest that Silvertop ever read this particular copy of *Truthteller* – or what his reaction was if he had – for the north east was in shock at the time following a terrible accident on 30 May at Stargate Pit, Townley, one of the collieries that Silvertop had leased to George Dunn. Thirty seven miners lost their lives, many of them from Stella. However, when the Squire finally reached London two months later he would certainly have been told about the *Truthteller* articles for another surprise awaited him at the annual meeting of the British Catholic Association on 1 June. According to *The Times*[3] after a Mr. French, described as a barrister, objected to Silvertop as a member of the Committee, alluding to his Newcastle speech, a 'scene of confusion ensued that baffles description, during which the terms "liar" and "coward" were applied to a gentleman present.' The following day *Truthteller* recorded the incident in almost similar terms in three paragraphs of a six-page report of the meeting[4], but in the issue a week later, Andrews was back with a two-pronged attack. Firstly, starting on the front page, there was an eight-page letter from himself to Edward Blount, secretary to the British Catholic Association, complaining at the outset that 'the Catholic name has been in some degree sullied by the want of decorum and candour' at the Association's meeting. He followed this with a long dissertation – 'without being chargeable with egotism' – of his personal experience in politics, which he claimed 'has been greater than most of my fellow Catholics.' He went on:

Without taking credit to myself, I do most sincerely wish that those individuals who first undertook the conducting of the affairs of the Catholic body, on the partial removal of the grievances affecting them in 1791, had been as honest towards the public as I have tried to be. How much scandal – how much jealousy – how much contention would have been avoided? Unfortunately, however, our affairs got into the hands of those who preferred secrecy and intrigue to openness and plain dealing – servility to independence – and court sycophancy to public opinion.

Before getting to the real crux of his letter, Andrews did reveal an interesting insight into what was going on. He said that one of those at the Association's recent meeting had let it be known that he had 'knowledge that there were individuals present who came with a predetermination to raise an opposition to the proceedings of the meeting.' However, he suggested that the gentleman was mistaken 'as there was clearly no concerted plan in the opposition that took place.' Then, addressing Edward Blount, he went on, managing once again to evoke the name of Dr. Milner:

I must now call your attention to the treatment experienced by Mr. French. From what I can gather there appears to me to be a strong private feeling between Mr. F. and some individuals of the same profession in the Committee, which I am sorry for; still this does not authorise the behaviour shown to Mr. F. which was far from being of the most decorous kind. This gentleman proposed a resolution relative to a member of the Committee, Mr. Silvertop, who is certainly not very popular in the Catholic body, in consequence of the ignorance he has evinced of the principles of his religion, and the indecent levity he has used in speaking of some eminent characters in the Catholic Church. I wish from my heart Mr. Silvertop would abstain from noticing religious doctrines and confine himself to political subjects. Mr. French moved that the Association was not responsible for the writings and speeches of Mr. Silvertop, building his motion, I presume, on the precedent set by the old Board in formally disavowing the *political* (they dared not the *theological*) writings of the late Dr. Milner ... why was he not permitted to proceed without interruption, or told that his motion was irregular? ... the expression of blasphemy, or something like it, imputed by Mr. French to Mr. Silvertop, was too pointed and strong; nevertheless it should not have been received with clamour and noisy vociferations.[5]

In the same issue of *Truthteller* there appeared a letter, signed by someone using the initials 'J.G.', who said as a member he had attended for the first time, the meeting of the British Catholic Association on 1 June and had been one of those who opposed Mr. French's motion, simply because if it had succeeded it would have fixed upon the Association a responsibility it never contemplated. However, he suggested that a measure of sever censure should have been moved against Silvertop.

> If Mr. S. considered a piece of irreverent jocosity would best chime in with his delighted wassailers – that his dissenting board mates would (in the ardour of having hooked a gudgeon) have cheered the highly-liberal Papist – if under the vinous influence of anti-popish sympathy, he thought he might make one among them by giving them a devil-may-care sort of speech, let him do so – but let him be prepared to expect that every good Catholic will condemn his folly, and rate his conduct as indecorous and disrespectful.

The writer went on to say that when he had read the reports of Silvertop's speech in Newcastle he could 'scarcely believe my eyes':

Is it to be borne, that this quack of the theological Squirearchy should spout out his idle and brainsick rhapsodies, without being called to severe account for them by persons of that Church, which he has falsely aspersed? Further, Sir, the consequences were to be looked to of letting this heretical assertion go unnoticed, falling from the lips of an apparent member of the Catholic community, at a time, place, and under circumstances, peculiarly and unhappily fitted to seriously injure and belie our cause, which rests on sound policy and Catholic Orthodoxy. How disastrous, Mr. Editor, would have been the effects of this indiscretion – this zeal for making ignorant speeches, had not your valuable *Truthteller* at once held up these odious and unfounded imputations to merited disgrace and perdition.[6]

As for George Silvertop's reaction to all this, we have only a passing reference in a letter written to John Lingard from Minsteracres in December 1826. After congratulating his old friend on his latest literary successes, the Squire remarked dryly: 'I think there is a party, of which Andrews is one, working to undermine the Association in London. They may do great harm, but I think they will not succeed.' [7]

References & Notes:

[1] Ward- Eve, vol. 2, p.182.
[2] *The Truthteller*, 22 April, 1826.
[3] *The Times,* 2 June, 1826.
[4] *The Truthteller,* 3 June, 1826.
[5] *The Truthteller*, 10 June, 1826.
[6] *Ibid.*
[7] Cambridge University Library, Add. MSS 9418/15/63.

Chapter Twelve

Jealousy and contempt

Alone at Minsteracres at Christmas 1826, Silvertop had plenty of time to ponder the events of the last year as his ageing mother was now in the habit of spending the festive season with her brother at Brough Hall, but whatever thoughts the Squire might have had on his vilification at the hands of Andrews and his cohorts, he did not share them even with his best friend Lingard. Instead, writing on Christmas Day itself, his letter was in response to Lingard's own momentous news. The English historian had become a particular favourite in Rome; in 1821 the previous Pontiff, Pius VII had conferred on him the triple academic laurel, creating him doctor of divinity and of canon and law, and in the summer of 1825, when Lingard paid his second visit to Rome, Pius' successor, Leo XII showed no less attachment to him, presenting him with a large gold medal as an extraordinary mark of his appreciation. Then, in October 1826, in creating new cardinals, Leo informed the consistory that among those he had reserved *in petto*[1] for the purple was 'one man remarkable for religion and piety, distinguished for learning drawn from original and authentic sources, who, *libris editio*, defends Catholic truth against heretics and schismatics, not less strenuously than successfully.' In Rome this was generally understood to refer to Lingard, for his *History* was then regarded 'as one of the great causes which had wrought such a change in public sentiment in England on Catholic matters.'[2] The humble vicar of Hornby, however, was quite happy where he was and when he heard the rumours he immediately wrote to Cardinal Litta, the Prefect of Propaganda in Rome, begging him, if the report were true, to use his influence with the Pope to divert him from his purpose. He also wrote on 15 December to his friend Silvertop seeking his advice, to which the Squire replied: 'This is much too grave a question for me to offer and opinion on' – and then promptly proceeded to do so:

> The whole twins on your own individual feelings of happiness. Will the dreadful restraints, the tedious pageantry, the banishment from England, suit the disposition of the Vicar of Hornby. Then, mindful of the politics of the Catholic Church, he added: I am afraid with the Vetoes of Austria, Spain & France, there is no chance ever for you, to the Tiara – but I think, if I did not feel disposed to accept the offer, I would at least let the offer be made. Assuredly it would be a proud renunciation & style, methinks, suited to your own happiness and independence.[3]

The Squire went on to more mundane news, telling his friend that the annual meeting of the local Catholic Association held in Newcastle earlier that month had been 'thinly attended – the Revs. Gillow & Crane & no other clergy – and very few Country Squires'; he commented: 'There is a most disgusting apathy in our Body & I verily believe that many of our Country Squires care not one sixpence about it.' (Silvertop had proposed a number of resolutions at the meeting, including one thanking the Vicars Apostolic for their Declaration of Catholic Principles drawn up earlier that summer). Then, obviously in a good humour, and referring to the possible offer of the bishopric to his friend, he signed off: 'Many, many returns of the Season to you – whether with the Hat, or without the Hat …'[4]

Three weeks later Silvertop was back in his favourite London hotel, the Clarendon in New Bond Street, to be greeted by a further assault on the leadership of the Catholic Association as a whole, in a letter published by the *The Truthteller* three days before the Association's annual meeting. The letter, on this occasion signed '*T.W., Hexham*', complained at length that the present Association, 'like all its *predecessors,* whether under the name of Committee, Board, &c, has invariably neglected to treat the Clergy with that respect and consideration to which, in the estimation of the public, they are justly and distinctly entitled.' The writer went on:

Where, then, originates their general indifference on the part of the Clergy? It requires no argument to prove that it arises from that pitiful jealousy which the lay members, and particularly the leaders of the Association, do, and always have, openly manifested towards the *Bishops* and the whole *Clerical Body*. They act upon all occasions as if they thought themselves *degraded* by *allowing* them any influence in conducting the affairs of the Association. This the Clergy have the sense to feel, as well as the manliness to spurn; and Mr. [Edward} Blount may be assured, that as long as their system continues to be pursued, the Association will find a very large proportion of the Clergy opposed to it, and consequently will make no progress in public opinion. The experiment of acting independently of the Clergy has been tried for many year, and has failed.[5]

Secretary Blount was the first to take issue with the writer of this particular letter at the Association's meeting in Thorney Street, Bloomsbury, three days later and was followed by one of the clergy present, the Rev. W. Morris, who said that he 'as a member of the sacred profession to which he belonged, spurned contemptuously, the interference of a man who, assassin-like, stepped forward under the cover of an anonymous signature, to throw his vile reproaches on the Association – a body to which all British Catholics were so deeply indebted.' He moved a resolution, seconded by another of the clergymen present and adopted by the whole meeting, denying the allegations. It was then the turn of Squire Silvertop, who said that as he lived near Hexham, where the letter was said to have come from, he could offer some facts that might be interesting on this occasion.

Not many months ago, a meeting of the Catholics of Northumberland was held in that county very respectably attended. One of the resolutions was a vote of thanks to the Vicars Apostolic for the declaration they had made respecting their tenets and principles. The Catholics of Northumberland knew the value of that document; but they had felt it during a severely contested. Another resolution of that meeting was a vote of thanks to the Association for the able address they had issued just previous to the election. A singular fact he would state, illustrative of the importance of that document – a copy of it was posted on the hustings at Alnick on the first day of the contest, and on the fifteenth days at three o'clock, it remained there untouched, thousands having, in the meanwhile, read it with admiration.' The Squire added that the meeting at which these resolutions were passed was held just a few miles from Hexham – 'no fact could more clearly prove that the Catholics in that neighbourhood did not share the feelings of the writer, who had impugned the Association.[6]

A report of the Association's meeting, together with the resolutions passed, was carried in the next edition of *The Truthteller*, but with the following rather sarcastic footnote:

The above account we have taken from the *Morning Chronicle*, not having a reporter present. Indeed, so little was thought of this meeting, that we did not think it worth our while to incur the heavy expense attending the employment of one of the Gentlemen of the Press on this occasion.[7]

Meanwhile, after his bruising encounter with his critics, George Silvertop decided to join Lord Stourton's younger brother, Edward Vavasour[8] on an extended tour of Europe, lasting several months and during his absence there emerged on to the Catholic stage in England a man who, even to this day, students of the period refer to as 'good Earl John', a man whose benevolence gave incalculable support to the forthcoming Catholic revival in England. That man was John Talbot, who at the age of thirty five, succeeded to the title and estates of his uncle Charles and became the sixteenth Earl of Shrewsbury and of

Waterford, with the rank of Premier Earl of both England and Ireland – a paradox for he could not sit in the House of Lords unless he publicly took an oath renouncing his religion. However, having inherited not only the intense devotion to the faith of his Catholic ancestors but also the long family tradition of abstention from political strife, the new earl was, for the moment, an impotent asset for those struggling against England's penal laws. But like a good many of the Catholic aristocracy who had kept the faith, the Talbots had also kept most of their large landed estates, and by any standards the sixteenth earl was a man of very substantial means which, in due course, he would employ to become a central figure in the great Catholic revival – and an inspiration perhaps to George Silvertop.

Shrewsbury's biographer Denis Gwynn[9], however, argues that John Talbot's supreme contribution to the revival was that he discovered the architect *extraordinaire*, Augustus Welby Pugin (1812-1852) when he was little more than a boy and before he became a Catholic, and that he made it possible for Pugin to devote his whole life and his prodigious energies and enthusiasm to the service of the Catholic Church. It is also worth noting that Talbot had been a dominating influence in the life of a young convert called Ambrose Phillips de Lisle, and that the three men, the new earl nearly twenty years older than the other two, eventually became so closely associated that it is said none of them can be thought of apart from the other two.[10] In the meantime, the new earl, just recently married, was more interested in completing the alterations begun by his predecessor at Alton, his principal seat (later to be called Alton Towers) in Staffordshire, and in any case, the spotlight of history focussed on another young man we mentioned earlier.

If nothing else, this was an age when the Church of England could boast it had a scholar and a gentleman in every parish, though it was more generally observed that so long as the latter qualification could be guaranteed the former might be overlooked. In the case of the parish of Brington, near Althorp, in Northamptonshire, as we have already noted, both these distinctions could be claimed with equal assurance. What else is known of the young vicar at Brington at this time comes from the pen of a Mrs Wykes, who knew him from childhood:

> His great charity to the poor and wandering beggars was unbounded. At times he gave them all the money he had, and stripped himself of his clothes to give them to the distressed; and when he had nothing to give, he would thank God he had only his holy truth to impart, and would speak of the love of God so fervently that he would call forth tears from the poor objects of

misery who came miles to beg money or clothes of him.[11]

She was, of course, talking of the Rev. George Spencer and the reason for re-introducing him into our story at this point is that after some years, by his own admission, of leaning towards Rome, it was in April 1827, that he first visited a Catholic priest[12], though his final conversion was another three years down the road. Spencer himself, however, was to place more significance on the arrival of three anonymous letters later that year, all in the same handwriting and all sent from Lille, recommending 'Rome' as the answer to his problems. It has never been revealed how she knew about Spencer's religious doubts though he did discover some time later that the author was a Miss Dolling, eldest daughter of a prominent English family who had been sent to Tournay to be educated, had converted to Catholicism and stayed on in Lille. She later joined the *Dames de Sacre Coeur* in Paris, but died during her novitiate, before she and Spencer could meet.[13] To the end of his life Spencer referred to Miss Dolling with gratitude as the one who had broken down his wall of prejudice and let in to his life the first gleams of Catholic faith.[14] Spencer's actual conversion, though, was the work of a young man referred to earlier, Ambrose Phillips de Lisle[15], who was ten years his junior. Spencer tells the story in his *Account of my Conversion:*

210

Near the end of the year 1829 I was introduced to young Mr Phillips, eldest son of a rich gentleman in Leicestershire, whom I had often heard of as a convert to the Catholic religion. I had been for a long time anxious to see him that I might observe the mode of reasoning by which he had been persuaded into what I still though so grave an error. We spent five hours together in the house of the Rev. Mr. (William) Foley, Catholic missionary in my neighbourhood, with whom I had already had much intercourse.

Spencer was clearly deeply impressed by his interview with the young theologian but not convinced.

He answered all my objections about his own conversion with readiness and intelligence. I could not but see that it had been in him the result of his own diligent investigations. I was delighted with what I could observe of his character. But yet my time was not fully come ... In a few days I again put aside the uneasiness which this meeting had occasioned.[16]

This meeting was the beginning of a lifelong friendship and it was after a weekend in January 1830, spent at Phillips' home with other Catholic personalities that Spencer wrote to his father announcing his conversion and within a week was received into the Catholic Church by Father Charles Caestryck, at Holy Cross Church in Leicester. Phillips, who after he had become a Catholic, had devoted his life to bringing England back to the 'Old Faith', described Spencer's conversion as 'a sign that God has grand designs on our wretched country.'[17]

Two months later George Spencer was on his way to the English College in Rome, where he was greeted by former Ushaw student Nicholas Wiseman, now rector of that venerable institution and one of the most notable personalities in Rome. Immersed in the scholastic and diplomatic atmosphere in Rome, however, Wiseman was scarcely aware of what was going on in England and it was his new student who was to be instrumental in setting him on a new path. Believing the rector's great talents were better suited working for the conversion of England, Spencer, with characteristic frankness, suggested 'he should apply his mind to something more practical than Syrian MSS, or treatises on geology, and that he would rather see him take up what suited a priest on the English mission as it then was.'[18] Both rector and student were destined to play significant roles, along with Phillips, in the great Catholic revival that lay ahead in England.

Meanwhile, news of Spencer's arrival in Rome spread quickly and within days he received a letter from a Miss Letitia Trelawney, who was in Rome with her father, Sir Harry Trelawney, who at seventy years of age, had received special permission to prepare for the priesthood. In view of his age special attention had to be paid to instructing Sir Harry and the Cardinal in charge had applied to the Passionists in Rome to supply a priest for this purpose. The man chosen was Father Dominic Barberi, then in his early thirties, who as a young lay brother had visions that his life was to be spent in apostolic missions far from Italy, especially in England. It was a strange choice, for Father Barberi could speak neither English or French and Sir Harry could not speak Italian, so it was upon hearing that Spencer had arrived in Rome, that the daughter wrote asking him to act as interpreter. As a result, Spencer became the first Englishman with whom the Passionist, harbouring a burning desire to convert England, had any intimate conversation[19]. Spencer introduced Father Barberi to his friend Phillips, who had accompanied him to Rome, and the two young converts seemed to personify all that the Passionist priest had dreamed of for years. We are now, however, getting well ahead of ourselves and must leave Spencer and Phillips with Father Barberi in Rome, for the moment, and return to 1827 and the travels of Squire Silvertop

Writing to his friend Lingard from Friborg, in Germany, on 4 August 1827, he said: 'Our tour has been most fortunate and it is now ringing to a close, as we intend to be at Geneva by the 12th and at Paris by the 24th' and urged Lingard 'if you have a vacant quarter of an hour' to write to him c/o Mrs Daisy Robinson, Paris. He told Lingard that his *History of England* was being advertised in various papers in Germany and that he had actually seen a copy of the final volume translated into German. He then reported that while dining at a hotel in Baden he had sat next to a gentleman who told him he had three grandsons being educated in England who enjoyed reading William Cobbett[20], Dr. Lingard and Sir Walter Scott. 'I assure you, I laughed most heartily at the idea of the company you were mixed up with.' As to the situation in England, Silvertop wrote:

> Every man on the continent speaks with absolute contempt of the conduct of our government to its Catholic people. I am afraid that things will come to great bitterness unless the King can be persuaded to agree to reason. For it is no longer a <u>Question of Reason</u> but a <u>Sign of Piety</u> and whenever that happens violence and bad passions are the certain consequence.

He said that he and his travelling companion had visited several churches where, while the priest was saying Mass, the people were singing the

Gloria and Credo in German, commenting 'I was very glad to see it.' The Squire ended by saying that he would be at Minsteracres in October and extended an invitation to his friend to visit.[21] In fact he arrived home with a group of friends on 19 September, to find an exciting invitation waiting for him from the secretary to the Protestant Bishop of Durham, Dr. William van Mildert. The following morning he replied:

> My Dear Sir - I reached this place (Minsteracres) last night, after a long Continental tour and not in very good health, and I really thought before opening your letter that I had come to anchor for at least three months. But the invitation of the Bishop of Durham is so flattering and my anxiety to pay my deepest of respects to the Duke of Wellington (from whom I have received many acts of great kindness) so great, that I try to assure you that I will have great satisfaction in obeying the summons, although I must leave Sir Henry Lawson and other gentlemen to take care of themselves. Nothing but ill health will prevent me appearing in person on the 3rd of October.[22]

Wellington paid a three-week visit to the North East that autumn, principally as the guest of his former adjutant-general, Lord Londonderry[23], at Wynyard Park, County Durham. He also spent a week with the Duke of Northumberland, at Alnwick, and attended civic ceremonies in Newcastle, Gateshead and Stockton. According to a report in the local Press, when Wellington arrived by carriage on the outskirts of Durham, the large waiting crowd unhitched the horses and proceeded to drag his carriage in triumph into the town centre to the accompaniment of church bells and a 21-gun salute from the castle. That night, according to the local newspaper, 'a more distinguished party has never, perhaps, been assembled in this county'[24] and Squire Silvertop was among the guests who sat down to dinner in the great hall in the Bishop's Castle. Sir Walter Scott, the novelist, was also there, and wrote in his diary:

> We dined, about one hundred and forty or fifty men; a distinguished company for rank and property ... in the rude old baronial hall, impressive from its antiquity...' After dinner they went to the Assembly Rooms. 'I saw some very pretty girls dancing merrily that old fashioned thing call a country-dance which Old England has now thrown aside, as she would do her creed, if there were some foreign frippery offered instead. We got away after midnight, a large party, and reached Ravensworth Castle – Duke of Wellington, Lord Londonderry, and about

twenty besides – about half past one. Soda water, and to bed by two.[25]

Perhaps understandably, Wellington's visit to the north east led to one of the more enduring of the Silvertop legends; that Britain's national hero had not only visited, but actually stayed a Minsteracres[26] and that the magnificent trees lining the drive, called 'Wellingtonians', were planted in honour of that visit – similarly the naming of the 'Wellington Pond' to the north of the house. Firstly, an actual visit to Minsteracres would hardly have gone unnoticed by the Press, both local and national, who diligently recorded his every move while he was in the north east. As for the trees (Latin name *Sequoiadendron giganteum*) they are native to the mixed coniferous forests of the central and southern Sierra Nevada in eastern California, and according to the Royal Forestry Society, were first introduced into Britain four years after George Silvertop's death, in 1853 (documentation exists suggesting the Minsteracres trees were planted in 1857[27]) and got their British name after the Iron Duke who died in the year (1852) of their discovery. The most famous avenue of 'Wellingtonians' is on the Duke 's former estate at Stratfield Saye, Hampshire.

References & Notes:

[1] Meaning 'in secret', the recipient's name to be released at a later date.

[2] Gillow, p. 254.

[3] In fact, Leo died soon afterwards, without having revealed the names of the cardinals he had elevated *in petto*.

[4] Cambridge University Library, Add. MSS 9418/15/64.

[5] *The Truthteller*, 27 January, 1827, pp. 125-128.

[6] *The Truthteller*, 2 February, 1827, pp. 166-168.

[7] *Ibid*, p. 168.

[8] Edward Stourton changed his name to Vavasour on inheriting the estate of an extinct Yorkshire family. In 1828 he was made a baronet.

[9] Denis Gwynn, *Lord Shrewsbury, Pugin and the Catholic Revival*, Hollis & Carter, 1946.

[10] *Ibid*, author's preface, p.xiv.

[11] Young, p. 29.

[12] *The Catholic Standard*, December 10, 1853, p. 6. Note: One of the Catholic priests Spencer was in contact with at this time was Father John Fletcher, D.D. a prolific author who in the early 1800s served at the mission in Hexham where he became a favourite of the Silvertop family (see Bannister-Rutter correspondence).

[13] Jozef Vanden Bussche, C.P., *Ignatius (George) Spencer*, Leuven University Press, 1991, p. 24.

[14] Young, p. 32.

[15] Ambrose Phillips de Lisle was the eldest son of Charles March Phillips of Garendon Park and Grace Dieu Manor, Loughborough, Leicestershire. He became a Catholic at the age of 16 while a student at Rev. George Hodson's school at Maisemore Court, near Gloucester. In 1826 he studied at Trinity College, Cambridge, and with a small core of others formed what became known at the university as the "Catholic Converts" who would cycle the 25 miles to St. Edmund's College at Old Hall, Ware, to attend Mass.

[16] Young, p. 36.

[17] Mark Bence-Jones, *The Catholic Families*, Constable, *1992, p. 147.*

[18] Wilfrid Ward *The Life and Times of Cardinal Wiseman*, London, 1912, vol. 1, p. 101.

[19] Denis Gwynn, *The Second Spring*, The Catholic Book Club, 1944, p. 36.

[20] William Cobbett (1763-1835) was a radical British politician and journalist who published the weekly *Political Register* (1802-35).

[21] Cambridge University Library, Add. MSS. 9418/15/65

[22] Durham University Iibrary, Van Mildert. 755.425.

[23] Lord Londonderry's second wife was Lady Frances Anne Vane-Tempest, coal heiress daughter of Sir Harry Vane-Tempest, of Seaham, County Durham.

[24] *Durham County Advertiser*, October 6, 1827.

[25] Sir Walter Scott's Journal, Edinburgh, 1927, p. 458.

[26] See *Evening Chronicle*, 23 September, 1954, p. 21.

[27] *Natural History Transactions of Northumberland and Durham*, 1873-1876, vol. v, p. 85.

The Rev. Thomas Gillow

He opened the
attack on Silvertop
and other leaders
of the national
Catholic campaign.

Chapter Thirteen

The Newcastle critics

If Squire Silvertop thought he had heard the last of his critics he was sadly mistaken. Christmas 1826, alone once more at Minsteracres, was again a time for reflection, only this year he was smarting from the memory of another unedifying encounter with critics – this time much closer to home, which, thanks to William Eusebius Andrews and *The Truthteller*, would subsequently cause him considerable embarrassment at national level.

Parliamentary reform, rather than emancipation, was now the focus of attention for the administration of an ailing Lord Liverpool and the Catholics were desperately searching for a means to revitalise their campaign on the political front. One of the ideas under discussion, one that had in fact emanated from the Newcastle Association the previous year, was for a levy of sixpence per individual to be collected in every chapel in the country to help meet the cost of publicising the Catholics' cause. And it was George Silvertop's introduction of a resolution in support of the idea at the annual meeting of the Newcastle Catholic Association at the Turks Head Inn on 19 December 1826 that prompted a heated confrontation with members of the clergy present. To make matters worse, they were men the Squire had known since their days at Douay College together. (In the absence of any other, we are forced to rely on a report of the meeting – much disputed later, as we shall see – as published by *The Truthteller*.)

First there was the Rev. Thomas Gillow, now missioner at Shields, who began by paying tribute to the eloquence of the Squire of Minsteracres, but then rounded on the leaders of the British Catholic Association as a whole, claiming they were not trusted by his fellow clergy. 'So long as that distrust exists I cannot consent to become active in the collection of money to be placed in the hands of individuals whom, I find, have not the confidence of either the Clergy or of the people,' he said. Gillow was followed by the Rev. E. Crane of Sunderland who said the distrust of the national Association ' is universal, and depend upon it, not without reason' and, finally, James Worswick, priest in Newcastle since 1795,[1] who joined the attack on the Association and its predecessor the Catholic Board:

> I am really apprehensive that the spirit and genius of that defunct Old Board survives in the New Association, and that it is their intention to pursue the same evil policy, and play the game of division and dissension. I entered this room without any feeling of hostility towards any individual, and none do I feel; but for what purpose, I ask, but that of insinuating, of hinting, and casting censure upon the clergy, and exciting popular odium against them, could that resolution be so strongly pressed upon this meeting?

Worswick, who was known as a bold, eloquent and animated preacher,[2] said it was 'absurd' to try and press the resolution when a country-wide appeal the previous year to the clergy for their reaction to the idea had been largely ignored.

George Silvertop immediately rose, saying he intended to treat with the utmost contempt the remarks of a man 'who thinks it absurd in any one to venture to dissent from him' but claimed his resolution was merely intended as a vote of thanks to the Committees of the British Catholic Association for their prompt adoption of the resolution that had been formulated by the Newcastle Association itself. After further discussion the resolution was finally carried by the meeting (the clergy members dissenting) but when Silvertop attempted to introduce a second resolution urging the national association to make its best efforts to put the proposal into effect, there was considerable confusion, during which a man who was not a member of the Association rose to address the meeting.

Charles Fox Larkin[3] (1800-1848), a surgeon, born at Ravensworth, Co. Durham, was the eldest son of an innkeeper. Sent to Ushaw College to study for the priesthood, he had decided to leave because of lack of vocation and turned instead to surgery. For many years while building a practice in Newcastle, he remained comparatively unknown, but in the latter years of the fight for emancipation he came to prominence as an eloquent public speaker and trenchant writer. On this occasion, he said, he was forced to speak despite not being a member of the Association, because of the 'wanton and unnecessary insult' offered to the Rev. Worswick by Mr. Silvertop.

> I cannot, Sir, restrain my indignation at such unworthy treatment, and I rise almost involuntarily to repel an insult offered to him without provocation, and before a company of gentlemen, the greater part of whom are members of his congregation. The word *absurd*, used by Mr. Worsick, seems to have given offence to Mr Silvertop. I conceive that he has

misunderstood the application of the epithet. He did not state that what Mr. Silvertop said, or that the resolution Mr. Silvertop had proposed was absurd.

At this point he was apparently interrupted by the Squire – 'Yes, Sir, he did'– who then went on to demand that the man had no right to speak as he was not a member, to which Larkin replied:

Gentlemen, when I rose I was prepared for this interruption, and should not have exposed myself to this indignity, had it not been for the purpose of vindicating Mr. Worsick, and giving expression to my resentment at the unworthy treatment of him by Mr. Silvertop, and in which you, gentlemen, by you silence, have participated. I will spare you the trouble of putting me down, but before I sit down I will make one observation. I cannot recognize, in this small number of men, however respectable you all may be, the Catholics of the two countries of Durham and Northumberland, nor can it be suffered that you should erect yourselves in to the Censors of the Clergy, or the Dictators of the people. What influence, think ye, can you possess over a body of men, numerous and intelligent, whom you exclude from your meetings, whom you will not suffer to participate in your discussions, and to whom you will not even submit your report and resolution for approbation or rejection? You will be conjurors indeed, if, treating them thus, you extract one penny from their pockets. To a domination of this aristocratic sort I am sure they have too much sense and spirit to submit, but least of all will they bend their necks to the haughty and imperious rule of one proud rich man.[4]

The report by *The Truthteller* ended by saying that 'at four o'clock the Gentlemen who attended the meeting sat down to an excellent dinner, and prolonged to a very late hour the festivity of the evening', adding (not surprisingly): 'None of the Clergy were present.' Now, clearly there must have been a bit more history to this bitter exchange between the Squire and the local clergy – the detail of which we are never likely to uncover – but when brooding over events at home that Christmas Silvertop would have drawn some comfort from the fact that it had always been the custom of the Newcastle Association to exclude members of the press so that their deliberations would remain private. On this occasion, however, he had clearly underestimated the wiles of his old foe, Mr. Andrews, for on his way down to London for the annual meeting of the national Association he stopped at a friend's house in Lancashire and was handed the latest copy of *The Truthteller* which, to his horror, he found contained a lengthy report of the Newcastle meeting. At least, it was a *version* of the proceedings, which began on the front page, preceded by a short editorial signed by Andrews himself, which read:

> Friends and Fellow-Believers – I lay before you a report which I have received of the proceedings of a meeting, purporting to be the annual meeting of the members of the Catholic Association for the Counties of Durham, Northumberland and Newcastle upon Tyne, to which I call your serious attention. Any note or comment from me, at least for the present, would be superfluous; the facts elicited speak for themselves. I cannot, however, refrain from observing, that the truly public-spirited conduct of the Rev. Mr. Gillow and the Rev. Mr. Worsick, and also of Mr Charles Larkin, entitles them to the heartfelt thanks of every one of us, and I trust this grateful feeling will be manifested by some public record of the Catholic body in this land.[5]

As to the accuracy of the accompanying report, Andrews prefaced each account of a speech with the words (in the case of the Rev. Gillow) '…spoke nearly as follows …', (in the case of the Rev. Crane) '…we profess to give nothing more than the substance …', and (in the case of the

225

Rev. Worswick) '...whose observations were to this effect ...'[6], although no such precaution preceded the words attributed to George Silvertop. Predictably, the *Truthteller's* report became the main topic of discussion at the packed annual meeting of the national Association in London on 21 January 1828 (we rely on this occasion on a report in the *Catholic Miscellany*). It began after the Association's secretary, Edward Blount, was asked by one of the clergy present whether its was true, as stated in *The Truthteller*, that 'a select committee had been formed out of the General Committee of the British Catholic Association; and that this chosen body of Vetoists sit in enclave at Norfolk House[7], for the purpose of arranging a Concordat at Rome', Blount replied that the statement was a 'malicious falsehood', adding:

> ...if he who conducts a public journal, makes it a medium for the propagation of falsehood, accepting with avidity and circulating without inquiry, and with manifest exultation, charges of the deepest dye, and which, if true, would blast with eternal disgrace those who are the objects of them as labouring to destroy what, by every tie, human and divine, they are pledged to uphold – if a public journalist will condescend to act such a part as this, make such charges on light grounds, and triumphantly bid for more by promises of

inviolable secrecy, he is a public pest, and every honourable mind will recoil with disgust from his polluted pages.

When George Silvertop finally rose to speak he began by saying:

Often as I have offered myself to the attention of these meetings, I never felt more acutely than I do on the present occasion because, Sir, the matter is of a personal nature and because the subjects, in some degree, relate to persons with whom I have always been on terms of civility and friendship. I had, indeed, Sir, made my mind completely up never more to appear at any Catholic meetings whatever, but reflecting on my pillow last night on that determination and having received two letters this morning from most valued friends requesting, most strongly, my attendance this day, I now appear to present myself to your indulgence because I thought, in the event of any remark being made on my character, or any allusion to the meeting lately held at Newcastle, the more manly course was to appear in the midst of my fellow citizens, engaged, as you are, in the attainment of our most glorious cause.

He said *The Truthteller* report contained allegations of. 'slight shown to the Catholic clergy, my conduct to Mr Worsick, and my having stated something relative to the marriage of the clergy', yet in the speech he was reported to have made there was not one word relative to the Catholic clergy.

> In the speech I did make, and in expressing my most anxious hope, as I now do, of a general plan of contribution being adopted, I did say, what I then, do now, and always have believed, that the Catholic clergy of England – a body of men who, for learning, for extreme attention to the wants of their flocks, for piety, and for every virtue that adorn human nature – were, if equalled, not exceeded, by any body of men in the world, would when they more maturely weighed this most important subject, give it their countenance and support. Again, speaking of one of my best of friends, the late Dr. Poynter, I stated, that the plan had the entire approbation and warm support of that most lamented prelate; whose virtues were well known and to whom no language of which I was master, could do justice.

He said *The Truthteller* had reported none of these remarks because, in his opinion, and that of his friends, the object was 'that of lowering me in the estimation of that body.' He went on:

> With respect to my conduct towards Mr Worsick, in my reply, I certainly did say to that reverend gentleman that I should give myself to the trouble to reply to his speech. And here, I beg that every gentleman present will put himself into my situation, having been from its beginning a member of the old Catholic Board, and of this Association; of that most calumniated Board I say which, whatever were the imperfections of its formation, had no other object in view than the furtherance of the Catholic cause. How would he like to hear, in a manner, the violence of which I will not endeavour to express, the exertions of many of the illustrious dead – of the Talbots, of the Dormers, of the Stourtons, of the Englefields, of the Throckmortons – denominated by the appellation of propagating discord, and distracting, and splitting in to factions, the Catholic body?

> Again I ask, by what possibility of construction can the resolution I moved at Newcastle be meant as a censure upon the clergy? No such idea ever came across my mind: to be accused of such intention was unjust, and unfair. Let any gentleman of

this Association – the nobleman, the clergyman, the lawyer, the merchant, the gentleman, giving as they do, their valuable time for the furtherance of our cause – ask himself how he would like to be accused of being about to play the same game of distracting and dividing the Catholic body. To such insinuations I did feel myself compelled to make the reply I did.

He then turned to his relationship with the Rev. Worswick, who in a subsequent letter to the Blount, the secretary, had apparently made some disparaging remarks about the Squire personally. Silvertop said he had known the Newcastle priest for many years and their relationship, he believed, had been one of 'civility and friendship'.

I am afraid, Sir, that day is gone by, for, in the answer to the admirable letter of our secretary, read this day, this reverend gentleman thinks proper to say of me, '... *with respect to Mr. Silvertop, this much, however, I will assert, that to my certain knowledge he has been taking unwarrantable liberties with the clergy, and sporting with religion at pleasure for more than five and twenty years'*. What line of conduct I may pursue due to this most desperate charge, I at present cannot say: this much, however,

I will declare, that it is a foul and abominable falsehood.

Silvertop said that at the Newcastle meeting he had spoken in reply to Mr. Gillow and had been followed by others who had begged the clergy present to state any reason for opposing the resolution he had proposed. Again, the *Truthteller* had failed to report any of this.

Now, with regard to the third charge, it is to me most disagreeable to enter upon it. While Mr. Larkin was suggesting the propriety of having three or four laymen of each congregation to collect the annual contribution, I was sitting within one of Mr. Worswick and Mr. Gillow, and on Mr Larkin remarking how much the clergy were employed, I said in conversation to Mr. Worswick, and Mr. Gillow, 'Oh! Yes, but you will have plenty of employment bye and bye, you will be getting wives and children: you see what they are doing in the Brazils? Sir, these observations were made by me in perfect good humour; indeed, two days before we had been laughing on the same subject with two clergymen who dined at my house. But, if playing the fool with one another, if quizzing now and then is to be classed among the crimes of life, let us at once have the re-establishment of the

Inquisition. When Mr Larkin sat down, the Rev. Crane rose and accused me of having offered an insult to the clergy by what I had stated; and in terms somewhat warm, stating that he owed the whole of his education to the generosity of my ageing and venerable mother, dilated at length on the subject.

The Squire then declared that no such idea of an insult had ever entered his head, and even if he had made an error of judgement, as the Rev. Crane had expressed a debt of gratitude to his mother, 'a generous mind would have endeavoured to throw the mantle of its protection over her offending, and thus unfortunate son.' Appealing to all those present at the meeting to judge him on the facts that he had presented, Silvertop added:

Dining the day before yesterday at the house of a noble lord, a gallant officer told us an anecdote. He said, during on of the battles of the Peninsular War two distinguished officers, now both of historic names quarrelled; they determined to give and to receive instant satisfaction, and rode up to a colonel commanding his regiment, whom they requested to see fair play. He listened for a moment to them; the battle was raging in all its fury, and said: By ----, my good fellows, you must be mighty gluttons, indeed, if you are not satisfied with what is going on! So, Sir, I say to the Catholics of England: if the abuse your religion and your cause has met with for centuries is not enough for you, I think you must be mighty gluttons indeed![8]

With that he declared that he would not be putting himself forward for re-election to any of the Associations' committees in future and promptly sat down. (The *Miscellany* carried a short postscript from the Squire saying that in the heat of the debate he had forgotten to say that as his remarks relative to the marriage of the clergy seemed to have offended the reverend gentlemen, he had no hesitation in stating publicly his sorrow for having used them.) Then, according to the *Miscellany*, before the meeting ended, Peter Andrews, son of *The Truthteller's* proprietor, rose to inform the meeting that his father's 'correspondent' in Newcastle was to blame for the offending report, that his father had not been able to attend the meeting himself and 'was, therefore compelled to rely on information received from his correspondent, and he had neither suppressed nor added to that information.' At the same time, he said, he was sure his father 'would feel it to be his duty, after the explanation that had been given, to lose no time in calling the public attention to the facts as they really occurred.' What George Silvertop might have thought about this veiled retraction on the part of *The Truthteller* we have no way of knowing, for writing to his old friend Lingard a week later, his only comment on these events was to say that there had been 'very disagreeable work in our Body', adding 'but I trust soon to be emancipated from all such proceedings.'

The Squire could not, of course, have known just how prophetic his words were – emancipation was just around the corner - or, indeed how true his other predictions were in the same letter to Lingard about, firstly, the King (George IV) '...it is not thought he will live a year', secondly, the Jesuits '...I do not think they will be permitted to stay there (in France) long,' or thirdly, Earl Grey '...he arrives this day, all eyes are looking towards him, and if he plays his cards well, I think he will be Prime Minister before two years are over.'[9] All of which proved to be correct, but before we consider the consequences of these events, and how they affected the Squire of Minsteracres, the last word on his Newcastle critics belongs to another of Silvertop's friends, the lawyer Charles Butler. Butler did not get a chance to speak at the meeting but instead wrote to the *Miscellany* saying he had wanted to rebut the 'heavy charges' levelled against the Association and the old Catholic Board by the priests at the Newcastle meeting and asked them to publish an outline of his speech. In a lengthy review of the work done by the Board and its successor, Butler said:

Let not the Board, or the Association, be inflamed by vague, general, undefined charges; by insinuations; by sly or sonorous ribaldry; let not the serious imputation of propagating contention, discord, and faction, and of meriting distrust, be fixed on them by such illaudable means. I now repeat the well-known Latin sentence I quoted on the only other occasion I have addressed the Association - *concordia parvae res crescunt, discordia maximae dilabuntur;* by concord the smallest things increase, by discord even the greatest fall to nothing.

Finally, saying that he had often been accused of proposing Dr Milner's expulsion from the Board, with Mr. Silvertop seconding the motion, he produced the minutes of the meeting of 29 May 1813, when the celebrated event occurred, and after reading that it was, in fact, Peregrine Towneley who had proposed the venerable doctor's expulsion, with Lord Stourton seconding the motion, Butler concluded: 'I shall not add another word.' [10]

References & Notes:

[1] The Rev. Worswick spent all of his forty eight years as a priest in Newcastle. He was instrumental in building St. Andrew's Church, in Pilgrim Street, Newcastle, which was opened on 11 February 1798, with the first celebration of Roman Mass in Newcastle since the Reformation. Further growth in Newcastle's Catholic population led to a decision in 1838 to build St. Mary's Cathedral in Clayton Street, Newcastle. Father Worswick was a leading member of the committee overseeing the project but died (1843) before the Cathedral was completed.

[2] W. Vincent Smith, *Catholic Tyneside*, 1930, p. 76.

[3] In 1836 Larkin published his own newspaper, called the *Newcastle Standard*. However, he was soon in debt and his newspaper ceased publication in April 1837 amid bailiffs and a blazing row the editor had with his priest, Father Worsick.

[4] *The Truthteller*, December 29, 1827.

[5] *Ibid.*

[6] *Ibid.*

[7] The London home of the Duke of Norfolk, premier Catholic Earl in England.

[8] *Catholic Miscellany*, February 1828, vol. IX, No. 74, pp.127-147.

[9] Cambridge University Library, Add. MSS, 9418/15/67.

[10] *Catholic Miscellany*, February 1828, vol. IX, No. 74 pp.

Chapter Fourteen

A mere practical expedient

Less than six months after his triumphant tour of the North East, Wellington had replaced Lord Goderich as Prime Minster and was facing up to increased tension in Ireland as a result of O'Connell's victory in the County Clare by-election (as a Catholic though he was barred from actually taking his seat). Rural Ireland, moving rapidly towards social collapse, was the scene of a passionate Catholic revival, and the Act of Union had turned Ireland into a domestic English problem at the very time when massive Irish immigration, particularly to the north west and to London, was transplanting that problem to English soil.[1] Wellington, who regarded Catholic Emancipation as a political rather than religious issue, suspected O'Connell's tactics were only the beginning of a campaign for partial separation of Britain and Ireland once more and that continued resistance to the Catholics' demands was therefore not only impractical but also dangerous. He had already taken precautions when forming his Cabinet, excluding anti-Catholic hard-liners – with the notable exception of the popular Home Secretary Sir Robert Peel - and had ended up with a 'mixed' government of 'Ultras'[2], liberals and some ex-Whigs. Watching wistfully from the sidelines,

George Silvertop, back in London, commented in a letter to his friend Lingard on 29 March 1828:

> It was expected that the Duke's Government would be a very strong one – it is said, in the House of Commons, to be the weakest that was ever known and Sir (Robert) Peel has lost ground.[3]

His comment about Peel losing ground was probably a reference to the fact that the Home Secretary's Protestant convictions were beginning to weaken. Support for the Established (Anglican) Church was the life-blood of Toryism and Peel was a dedicated Tory. It was only two years previously that he had refused to join the government of George Canning, a long-time friend of the Catholics, because Canning made it clear he planned to introduce an Emancipation Bill. The Duke of Wellington had taken a similar stance, but O'Connell's subsequent activities had changed everything. Wellington knew he could not win a vote on emancipation without Peel's support and managed to convince his Home Secretary of the necessity, if not the desirability, of giving way on the Catholic question. (In fact, Peel proved to be the most important man in the House of Commons between 1828 and 1830, almost single-handedly sustaining Wellington's government in Commons' debates, while suffering a savage campaign of ridicule and abuse in the press for his own personal betrayal of Protestantism.)

Even with Peel's support, however, the Duke still faced the problem of George IV, an obese and irritable hypochondriac of sixty-seven, who following the death of the Duke of York, his favourite brother, had been very much under the influence of the fifth of the royal dukes, the sinister Duke of Cumberland, Grand Master of the (Protestant) Orange Society. When Wellington finally went down to Windsor in the spring of 1829 to present his cabinet's advice and to ask that the royal ban on their dealing with the Catholic question be lifted, the King was reluctant and is said to have sworn volubly as the details of the scheme were presented. In the end he gave his consent – only to change his mind six days later just as the first reading of the Bill was about to be presented to the Commons. Again Wellington went down to Windsor and this time, according to Ward,

> The King talked for six hours. The Duke never witnessed a more painful scene. He was so evidently insane. He had taken some brandy and water before he joined them, and sent for some more, which he continued to drink during the conference. During six hours they did not speak fifteen minutes. The King objected to every part of the Bill. He would not hear of it.[4] The very

next day, however, he relented and gave his ascent.

It was then up to Peel to persuade Parliament, and his four and a half hour speech in the Commons on 5 March 1829, was more a justification of his own actions than a presentation of the First Reading. More importantly for England's Catholics, however, he carried the day with a majority of 188. (The Duchess of Richmond invited the whole of Wellington's cabinet to dinner following the passing of the Act, but when they arrived, they found the dining room 'decorated' with two hundred stuffed rats -- an expression of the duchess' opinion of the government. Arguably, Peel spent the rest of his political life attempting to live down this 'ratting' on the constitution.) After the Bill received royal assent (April 13, 1829) Peel was denounced as a traitor by the Ultras and felt it his duty to resign his Oxford seat and give his constituents the chance to express their opinion of his *volte-farce*. They did and he was ignominiously and decisively defeated, his opponents taunting him with a rhyme - reprinted in the *Birmingham Argus* in January 1829 – that was to haunt him for many years:

Oh Member of Oxford, you shuffle and wheel

> You have altered your name from R. Peel
> to Repeal.

Ironically, among those who played an active role in Peel's downfall was a young tutor at Oriel College, Oxford, by the name of John Henry Newman, who features again later in our story. For the moment it is sufficient to record that Newman wrote to his mother:

> We have achieved a glorious victory. It is the first public event I have been concerned in and I thank God from my heart both for my cause and its success. We have proved the independence of the Church ...[5]

Wellington, meanwhile, immediately set about exacting spiteful penalties for his own grudging surrender; the '40-shilling freeholders'[6] of Ireland, for example, were deprived of the vote by the raising of the property qualification to £10 a year – in effect a disenfranchisement of all those people in Ireland likely to vote for O'Connell and his supporters. But Wellington too was to face public opinion when George 1V died the following year (*The Times* wrote 'there was never an individual less regretted by his fellow creatures than this deceased king') forcing a general election, the first in which Catholics were entitled to stand. Wellington was defeated and in the new parliament the Northumberland peer

Earl Grey headed a Whig administration with Catholics – for the first time - representing five English constituencies. It was left to Charles Butler, in his *Memoirs,* to honour the Duke's sacrifice:

> It was an arduous achievement. To affect it required the mightiest arm in the universe, that arm was the Duke of Wellington's, and he raised it in favour of the Catholic cause. Conqueror in India, conqueror in Spain, conqueror even of Napoleon, a nobler enterprise yet awaited him, and nobly did he soon afterwards achieve it.

There is little doubt that Catholic emancipation, marking the beginning of the end of the reign of privilege, was the victory of one man, more so perhaps than any other change of equal importance in history, but that man was not Wellington; it was Daniel O'Connell. Without O'Connell some further relief to the Catholics would no doubt have been conceded in time,

> but it would have been conceded as a boon granted by a superior to an inferior class, and it would have been accompanied and qualified by the veto. It was the glory of O'Connell that his Church entered the Constitution triumphant and unshackled – an object of fear and not of contempt, a

power that could visibly affect the policy of the empire.[7]

James Losh, a Unitarian barrister from Newcastle, noted in his diary for May 1829 the 'the country is tranquil, and Catholic Emancipation is, I have no doubt, gradually producing the happiest effects.'[8] No record exists, unfortunately, of Squire Silvertop's reaction to the Catholics' final victory – the cause that had dominated the better part of his adult life, though there can be little doubt he would have rejoiced with his co-religionist friends in singing his *Nunc Dimittis*[9]in thanksgiving. The sobering fact is, however, that while Catholic emancipation came to be regarded as one of the great liberal achievements of English statesmanship, it was at the time not so much an act of altruism, more a practical expedient. Perhaps that is why, in the only Silvertop letter to survive from that summer, there is no mention of it at all. On 29 June that year, the Squire was writing from his London hotel to another friend, William Salvin, member of a well-known Catholic family from Croxdale in County Durham, who were related by marriage.[10] In a letter uncharacteristically full of frivolous gossip, Silvertop begins with the fact that he has

never known anything equal to the number of invitations for dinner – to such a degree that I have not a day to myself till

I leave town, which will be the middle of next week.' He then added: 'The Breakfast on Saturday went off most wretchedly – it rained nearly the whole day – I did not go – but about three thousand persons went and all say it would have been most beautiful had the rain not come.

The Times of the same day reveals for us that the event he was referring to was the anniversary breakfast of the Horticultural Society, an occasion that, according to the newspaper report '… forms one of the principal attractions of the fashionable season, and is looked forward to with more anxiety than any other fete, either public or private…' Confirming Silvertop's account of a rain-sodden occasion, *The Times* reported it to be

what our neighbours beyond the Tweed call a 'drawky day', adding that, though the weather destroyed all that pleasure that would have arisen from seeing several hundreds of fine women, elegantly dressed, displaying their grace, either in the promenade or the dance, we doubt whether even the ladies themselves did not derive greater pleasure from the consciousness of the admirable temper and good-humoured endurance with which they bore their disappointment.

244

The Squire himself, still a bachelor at fifty-five years of age (and destined to remain so) gives the impression in his letter to Salvin that the possibility of marriage could have been on his mind, for having just mentioned that the King had a large party staying with him for the Ascot race, he inexplicably adds:

> I cannot tell you of a single (happy?) Catholic marriage. Poverty seems the general plea. However, there are many sighing young ladies - & some very pretty ones.[11]

To return to more mundane matters, however, it seems that those who believed that the 1829 Act would put an end to all agitation were to be sadly disappointed. The feeling against 'papists' was too indelibly engrained in the minds of the nation to be eradicated at once by a single Act of Parliament.   As for the Catholic community in England – no more than about one percent of the population – the fact that they were now emancipated brought no immediate benefit and in any case, everyone's attention had already turned to the quest for parliamentary reform.[12] For George Silvertop and six other leading Catholics around the country there was at least the honour of being selected as the first 'papists' to occupy the position of High Sheriff in their respective counties for more than 200 years. Named in the *London Gazette* of 12 November

1830, the seven were: Silvertop (Northumberland), Peregrine Towneley (Lancashire), Sir Edward Smythe (Shropshire), Thomas Fitzherbert (Staffordhire), Charles Eyston (Berkshire), Sir Henry Tichborne (Hampshire) and Sir Thomas Stanley (Cheshire). Their year in office was overshadowed, however, by tensions caused by the fall of the Bourbons in the 1830 French Revolution and the struggle between Grey and Wellington over parliamentary reform. When the Whigs came to power under Grey following the death of George IV in 1830, they agreed with the Radicals on the need for parliamentary reform but had no wish to establish democracy. While the latter wanted to give the vote to the working class, the Whigs would not extend it beyond the middle class. Wellington and the Tories, on the other hand, had pledged themselves to oppose reform to the last ditch.

As the politicians argued, a new movement sprang up, first in Birmingham, led by a wealthy banker called Thomas Attwood, a Radical. Called a Political Union, it was made up of middle and working class reformers who supported Grey, and the following summer a similar society was organised in Newcastle by Attwood's brother Charles, a glassmaker from Gateshead. Silvertop was a keen Grey supporter and undoubtedly Radical by inclination, but - probably because of his position as High Sheriff at this time – there is nothing to indicate his involvement with this

246

new movement, called the Northern Union. Luckily for Silvertop, while unrest grew in other parts of the country, northern country districts remained relatively calm and one of the highlights of his year as High Sheriff was the ceremonial opening of the 370-foot Scotswood suspension bridge across the Tyne, three miles west of Newcastle, on 12 April 1831. It was a spectacular affair, with a procession of between 80 and 90 carriages and over 5,000 onlookers, many on horseback. The mile-long procession, led by a military band and with the High Sheriff's carriage and four at its head, approached the bridge from the Northumberland side watched, according to the local press reports, by 'many thousands of anxious spectators.' The report went on:

> On entering on the bridge, by a precaution which was afterwards proved to be unnecessary, the carriages passed over at a considerable distance asunder; and when the carriage of the Rector of Ryton (the Rev. C. Thorp) approached the centre it was stopped and the blessing of Heaven on that bold and important work of man was most reverently and feelingly invoked by that reverent and respected individual.

On the other side of the bridge – the Durham side - the procession was met by the High Sheriff of Durham County Charles Clavering, on horseback, who accompanied it on a short circular route through his county and back to the bridge where it passed over for the second time, this time in closer order. Then, according to the Press, the bridge

> ... was soon after put to a much severer test, for as soon as the procession had passed over, the gates being opened, the crowds of people who had been previously assembled at each end, rushed, with thoughtless impetuosity, on to the bridge, in the centre of which they soon collected into so dense a mass as to be incapable of moving, and putting the bridge to a trial much more sever than in ordinary circumstances it can ever be exposed to again.

After the ceremony on the bridge the officials and invited guests retired to the Assembly Rooms for a dinner hosted by the Mayor of Newcastle, Archibald Reed. Proposing the toast of thanks, High Sheriff Silvertop said that as he was connected to Newcastle by birth and early association, he was greatly in favour of anything that brought happiness and increased commerce to its people, and he praised the Mayor and the corporation of Newcastle – 'enthusiastic admirers of improvement of every description' - for their support for the bridge project.[13]

A few miles to the west, at Stella, crossing the Tyne remained a constant problem, particularly for Catholics wishing to attend Mass on a Sunday. Prior to 1831 Mass was said in the chapel at Stella Hall where another of George Silvertop's nephews, Father Thomas Witham, was chaplain to Mrs George Dunn. It was Mrs Dunn who contributed the major portion (£950) of the cost of building a new Catholic church at Stella (George Silvertop contributed £100) and which opened in October 1831.[14]

Meanwhile, there was 'a powerful sensation' throughout the North East when the Commons passed the second reading of the Reform Bill by, but feelings quickly darkened when the Lords rejected it. There were riots in Bristol and Nottingham and protest meetings in Newcastle, Sunderland, Durham, Gateshead and other places.[15] In the same week as the opening of the Stella Church, Silvertop's duties as High Sheriff put him in the chair at a packed meeting in the County Court at Morpeth, north of Newcastle. Among the speakers was Silvertop's brother Henry Witham, who made a rousing speech, attacking the 'factious, unconstitutional and corrupt boroughmongers' in the Lords who had disdainfully rejected the Bill already passed by the Commons. He went on

> We must tell the House of Lords, in firm but constitutional language, before it is too late, that they must surrender their

parasitical privileges that have too long been fed and nourished on the heart's blood of the British Constitution![16]

A month later Silvertop attended another meeting of pro-reformists, this time in the County Courts at Durham, chaired by his counterpart Charles Clavering, High Sheriff of Durham County.[17] Addressing the gathering, Silvertop called for support for the administration of 'my venerable friend and brother Northumbrian, Lord Grey' and praised the new king, William IV, for resisting attempts to turn him against the principles of reform. He went on:

> During the last month it is well known that a system of cabal has been going on to poison his Royal mind against his advisers and the Bill, but our glorious monarch has remained immovable as a rock

He said events in France and the impoverished condition of the labouring classes as a result of the July revolution, were the best arguments he could use against the consequences of national convulsion, adding:

> I call revolutions calamities, for I was educated in the midst of the most bloody that ever occurred – they spare neither rich nor poor but, like the scythe of death,

250

sacrifice the high and the low. No statement in history, I believe, is more true than that if the governing few continue for a long period to resist the wishes of the governed many, revolution is near at hand.[18]

It was another eighteen months before the Lords finally passed the Reform Bill (April 1832, by nine votes), a turning-point in modern English history but the celebratory bell-ringing and banquets were overshadowed by a winter of discontent brought about by food shortages, mass unemployment, and the worst kind of working class revenge imaginable – cholera. Sweeping through Europe from the Middle East, it was the classic consequence of rapid urban growth creating unsanitary living conditions, and the disease arrived on the British mainland at Sunderland in October 1831. Once Newcastle had been affected (27 November) it acted as the hub and with domino affect, struck villages along both banks of the Tyne, as well as many of the colliery villages that dotted the Durham and Northumberland landscape. By February 1832 almost the whole of the North East of England was affected and failure to impose sanitary cordons or to restrict trade from the infected areas meant that the disease had by then reached London. No record exists to reveal whether anyone living on the Minsteracres estate was affected but according to the Official Cholera

Returns of Great Britain there were 71,508 cases of cholera and 26,101 deaths in Britain (excluding London) between October 1831 and December 1832. Newcastle suffered over 400 deaths while London at first appeared to have escaped relatively lightly but a second wave began in the May 1832 and by December 9,172 cases had been recorded in the capital resulting in 4,281 deaths.[19]

Notes & References:

[1] W.R.Ward, *Religion and Society in England 1790-1850*, B.T.Batsford Ltd., 1972, p.115. An Oxford-trained historian, Ward was for many years a member of the Department of History at Manchester University, then Professor of Modern History at the University of Durham.

[2] Protestant right-wing Tories.

[3] Cambridge University Library, Add. MSS 9418/15/66.

[4] Ward – Eve, vol. iii, pp. 309-311.

[5] Robert Sencourt, *The Life of Newman*, London, 1948, 1, p. 44.

[6] Established by an act of 1430, the '40-shilling freeholder' granted the right to vote to all those who owned property with a rental value of at least 40 shillings per annum. In Scotland the figure was £100, excluding the great mass of the population.

[7] W.E.H. Lecky, *History of Ireland in the Eighteenth Century*, London, 1892.

[8] *Diaries & Correspondence of James Losh,* edited by E. Hughes, Surtees Society vols. 171-174 (1956/9).

[9] *Nunc Dimittis* (Luke ii, 29-35) is divided into two parts, the first a prayer to God (liturgically this alone came to be designated the *'Nunc Dimittis'*) and the second a prophecy spoken to Mary.

[10] William Salvin's daughter Anna Maria was married to George Silvertop' s nephew, William Witham (Henry's son) whose sister Winefred later married Gerard, another member of the Salvin family.

[11] Durham Country Record Office, D/Sa/C 147.

[12] The origins of the electoral reform movement can be traced back as far as the seventeenth century, but it was in the 1760s, in London, that the movement first started to achieve mass support. The example of the French Revolution boosted demands for reform, but it was not until the economic slump of 1829-30 drew together diverse critics of the unreformed system in a new challenge to the principal objectors, the Tories, that the movement finally gained a firm footing.

[13] *Newcastle Weekly Chronicle,* 16 April 1831.

[14] *Newcastle Weekly Chronicle*, 15 October 1831.

[15] S. Middlebrook, *Newcastle upon Tyne, its* Growth *and Achievement*, Kemsley House, 1950, p. 174.

[16] *Newcastle Weekly Chronicle*, 15 October 1831.

[17] Three hundred Northern Union members from Newcastle, led by Attwood, marched to Durham to prevent the Marquis of Londonderry and his 'lambs', i.e. the Durham Yeomanry, from breaking up the meeting.

[18] *Newcastle Weekly Chronicle,* 5 November 1831.

[19] Michael Durey, *The Return of The Plague,* Gill and Macmillan, 1979.

Minsteracres (north view)
mid nineteenth century

This is the house as it was during
George Silvertop's lifetime,
before the addition of the
ballroom, parlour
and church by his heir
Henry Charles (Englefield) Silvertop
in the late 1850s.

The Staircase Room

As it was in George Silvertop's day,
featuring figurines by the
artist-turned-sculptor John Lough
on either side at the top of the stairs.

Holy Cross Church, Ryton

Burial place of the majority of
the original Silvertop family.
George (1774-1849) was
the last to be buried
in the family crypt, which lies
beneath the chancel in this
Anglican church at Ryton.

Henry Charles Englefield
1826-1887

Four years after this sketch was drawn young
Englefield inherited the Minsteracres
estate, at the age of twenty three. His mother
was the daughter of George Silvertop's brother, Henry.

Published by kind permission of John Trappes-Lomax

The squalor of London's 18th cent. streets

Chapter Fifteen

Back home to Minsteracres

London is a city with a reputation for death and violence stretching back as far as any written records; quite apart from the plagues and great fires, few would wish to recall, for example, that in 1189 the coronation of Richard I was marked by the wholesale murder of Jews – men, women and children burned and cut to pieces. Later a 'diversion' to be witnessed in the capital, according to many reports, was female combat, in which women fought to the death, naked, with two-handled swords, while in the 1830s, quite apart from the everyday robberies, assaults and manslaughters amidst the squalor that lay behind a few select streets, London was being terrorised by 'Spring-Heeled Jack', a monstrous figure by all accounts in a white oilskin suit and long black cloak who belched blue flames as he ripped at his victim's clothing – mostly women – with metal-like claws. Indeed, anyone reading Peter Ackroyd's *London the Biography,*[1] would be excused for wondering why George Silvertop chose to spend so much time in the capital, away from the security, peace and tranquillity of Minsteracres. Perhaps it was that he felt akin to Joseph Addison, who wrote in the *Spectator* of July 1711:

> I shall therefore retire to the Town, and get into the Crowd again as fast as I can, in order to be alone.

Probably not an attraction for George Silvertop, but there is that more popular myth associated with the metropolis wittily illustrated by the famous early-nineteenth century cartoon of two men meeting beside a London milestone. One, returning from the city, is bowed and broken; the other, advancing upon him full of animation and anticipation, shakes his hand and asks: 'Is it paved with gold?'[2] More interesting for the purposes of our story, however, is London's association with the novelist Charles Dickens

(1812-1870). In real life Dickens was no stranger to the city; he enjoyed a long friendship with one Baroness Burdett-Coutts, the multi-millionairess granddaughter of Coutts, the banker, and their usual rendezvous in the 1830s was the Clarendon Hotel in New Bond Street, where George Silvertop had become almost a permanent resident over the years. Run by a Frenchman called Jacquier, who had been chef to Louis XVIII, the Clarendon was famous for its French dinners, which could cost, including a bottle of wine, as much as four guineas.[3] Unfortunately, apart from mention of the celebrated breakfast attended by three thousand people (previous chapter) the only other reference to any kind of social life in London unconnected to his interest in religious affairs, is to be found in Silvertop's letter to Charles Butler, describing his meeting with Napoleon, when he says he told the Emperor

> I had the good fortune to be admitted to the private society of His Royal Highness. (See Appendix 2).

That was in 1814, of course, during the second half of the reign of George III, the 'mad' King, and Silvertop was most probably referring to the Royal circles surrounding the then Prince of Wales (later George IV). Whether he enjoyed the same *entrée* to that dazzling level of society in subsequent years we have no way of knowing, but in any case, there was to be a dramatic change in his lifestyle soon after his term of office as sheriff came to an end. There was considerable distress throughout the country during the winter of 1831-32, the suffering caused by the cholera epidemic intensified by mass unemployment and chronic food shortages, and the situation became even worse when, in May 1832, the Lords again rejected Grey's Reform Bill, raising the spectre of civil war. Grey was particularly popular in the north[4] and when he subsequently resigned threats of violence were made against the Duke of Northumberland, Lord Londonderry, Lord Redesdale, the bishop of Durham and other peers who had voted against the bill. On his way back from London to his seat, Howick Hall, in Northumberland, that summer, Grey was enthusiastically greeted in every town he passed through in the north[5]. The crisis was averted two months later when the King gave assent to the Bill and promised to create enough new peers to ensure its success through the Lords, resulting in widespread rejoicing in the north. Bonfires were lit and dinners arranged to celebrate 'the triumph of the people' despite the fact that it was a very limited triumph, for the bill made no revolutionary changes. Prior to 1832 the franchise in Newcastle had been restricted to freemen[6], of whom there were some 3,000 out of a total population of 53,613 in 1831; under the new uniform £10 householder franchise the number of voters reached just short of five thousand, less than one-tenth of the number of inhabitants. What the bill did achieve, however, was to limit the opportunity for direct bribery in elections.[7]

No sooner had life begun to return to normal in 1832 than further unrest erupted as a result of the miners of Durham and Northumberland trying to establish a trade union. The previous year the owners had been forced to concede to the miners' demands for better conditions after a ten-week strike but the employers' determination to break the union led to a second strike lasting four months, during which union leaders and their families were forcibly ejected from their homes. A local magistrate was brutally murdered near Jarrow Slake and of the strikers was shot by a policeman. Towards the end of August privation forced the men to yield and the subsequent victimisation of their leaders broke up their organisation.[8] All of this would have been particularly distressing for the Silvertop family, with their long and close association with the coal mining industry, but there was even greater sadness for George Silvertop with the death of his friend Charles Butler, aged eighty one, and a few months later his mother, Catherine aged eighty five. No correspondence exists from this period, but there is evidence to suggest that as a result of his mother's passing the Squire spent much less time away from Minsteracres. We know that he decided to provide a much larger chapel for the local Catholic community, moving it from inside the house (in the room presently used as a library) to a room upstairs in the outbuildings.[9] This was in 1834, the year Joseph Aloysius Hansom (a young architect with an engineering flare) was making a name for himself in London with his 'Patent Safety Cab' (20 years later he would design St. Elizabeth's Church at Minsteracres). The Squire's namesake, the Rev. George Silvertop (a great, great nephew) refers to the new chapel and other alterations in his *memoirs:*

> In his father's time the drive came up on the south-east of the house, bringing you to the front entrance, then opening on to a large hall in the centre of the house. This as far as one can gather was the present staircase room. George Silvertop carried this drive, instead, round the back of the house (i.e. the west) and built a new entrance for it on the south side, with a colonnade adjoining the former chapel.[10]

The Rev. Henry Rutter had long since left - in 1823, after nearly forty years as resident chaplain – first by the Rev. Thomas Douthwaite (1823-39), then by the Rev. Edward Brown (1840-42) and finally by the Rev. John Rogerson[11] (1842-53) who was ordained at Ushaw. An eloquent preacher, he was also a keen huntsman and expert marksman with the gun. Meanwhile, commenting on the weddings and baptismal entries made by the Rev. Douthwaite in the Minsteracres register, the Rev. Silvertops wrote:

> We notice names of Catholics living far away from Minsteracres, e.g., at Corbridge, Mickley, Ebchester, etc. We must not forget that at that time the Catholic Missions were few and far distant from each other. At this point it will not be without interest to glance over the whole of Northumberland and see the state of the Catholic Church there at that epoch – a very important one in history, for it was the time at which Catholic Emancipation after so many hard struggles, had at last been granted by, or rather, forced upon the Government. What was its effect in the north in the first decade? First by consulting the *Catholic Directory* of the years 1825 to 1839, we see that the number of Missions remained stationary; for the whole of Northumberland there were fifteen or sixteen Missions: one of them only, Newcastle, was very important; another one, Hexham, had some importance but was rapidly declining; all the others were small scattered Missions: Alnick, Bellingham, Berwick, Biddlestone, Callaly Castle, Cheeseburn Grange, Ellingham, Felton, Haggerstone Castle, Longhorsley, Minsteracres, North Shields, Swinburn, Thropton. Two facts appear at

once: the Irish Immigration was only beginning and it was directed towards Newcastle and the surrounding district; so we see the venerable Fr. Worswick of St. Andrews striving in every way possible to enlarge his poor chapel in order to admit his growing congregation. But – and this is the second fact – in the country districts there was no increase in the Catholic population. There are many reasons to account for this: first, the population of the countryside was already beginning to flow to the industrial centres, the priests were few, their flocks scattered and living too far away to be properly cared for. The Catholics were hardly able to attend their churches; mixed marriages had a baleful effect; Catholics were looked down upon, despised, even often the victims of violent treatment; but the chief reason was that the Catholics had for so long been kept down by persecutions and penalties of all sorts that they could hardly convince themselves that a period of comparative freedom had come for them. They were living in perpetual fear that it was no more than a temporary alleviation of their sad state, and they were only too pleased to be able to practise their religion as quietly as possible.[12]

Meanwhile, the three generations of Silvertops who had resided at Minsteracres to this point had all been served – in the capacity of farm steward - by corresponding generations of a family called Swallow and in 1835 a new male member of that family was born on what was called 'home farm,' i.e., that part of the estate not tenanted. Named Thomas, he grew up during the final years of George Silvertop's life and eventually (1905) penned what he called *Reminiscences* of his childhood:

George Silvertop was ...an up to date agriculturist, and as a landlord had few equals in consideration to his tenantry. As an instance he would take a portion of his tenant's farm and add it to the home farm under the superintendence of my father. It was then thoroughly cultivated, and when in excellent condition, would be returned to the tenant. One farmer who was so treated assured my father that the produce of that portion paid the whole of his rent. Corn was one of the main products of the home farm and on the harvest being completed there was the inevitable 'kairn supper', an event eagerly looked forward to by old and young. The supper consisted of a plentiful supply of roast beef and plum pudding, etc. The company then went to the ball held in the large dining room in the Hall. The Squire and his aristocratic visitors always joined in the dance, begun with the time-honoured 'Keel-Row' (Country Dance). It was pleasing to observe that caste made no distinction of partners, for the aristocrat would co-mingle with the plebian – all were equal on these occasions. It is in the recollection of the writer that amidst the hilarity when the triumph was being played, a sudden stop of the music took place, when Mr. Silvertop, in a stentorian voice, shouted 'Play up, Bob!' (the musician for many years) he replied that 'The strings brocken, sor.' After repairs were affected the dance was resumed, and only ceased in the small hours of the morning, when the harvest people wended their way homewards, satisfied with their enjoyment and anticipated the next annual treat.

Recalling the school that George Silvertop established at Minsteracres – 'its four white-washed walls with no pretension to architectural design' – Swallow went on:

> The master used to take the boys into the fields to teach us practical land surveying, using the usual instruments. After taking the necessary measurements we returned to the school to calculate the area for our lessons. On the estate was kept a pack of

hounds, and on hunting days Mr. Silvertop would call and ask the master to let us follow the hounds, certainly to our great gratification. Happy were our school days!

Finally Swallow recalled the young local men that the Squire had helped 'by giving an opportunity of improving their position':

Mention may be made of a few who had the good fortune to benefit by his generosity, viz.: J.G.Lough, who worked as a stonemason in the neighbourhood of Minsteracres, who ultimately became famous as a sculptor. The two sons of his gamekeeper, Thomas and John Bewick, the former became a civil engineer of repute, the latter reached the position of a bishop. He also sent T. Swallow (a son of his head gardener) to the Botanical Gardens, London, where he became an expert in his profession, and he sent T. Elliott, a son of his estate carpenter, and R. Emmerson, tailor, to London for improvement in their respective trades, but on returning to the North the latter took up a more lucrative employment than using the needle. He sent a son of his butler to Ushaw College but he, the son, was never ordained as a priest. Mr. Silvertop made a generous proposition to my father, viz.:that he would put the three elder sons to trades and set them up in business, my father having to do for the other three; death, however, prevented him from carrying out his generous proposition.[13]

It sounds as if life at Minsteracres could have been almost idyllic at this time, but in reality disappointment among the working classes at their failure to win the franchise in 1832, fanned by a renewal of general distress, led to a revival of Radicalism throughout the country in the form of a mass revolt against living conditions which were almost unendurable. Such were the conditions that drove the wage earners under Radical leaders to believe that giving the working man the vote and allowing him to sit in parliament would provide the key to material wealth. So in 1838 William Lovett, a London cabinet maker, drafted the People's Charter, with its six demands: manhood suffrage, vote by ballot, the abolition of the property qualification for M.P.s, payment of members, equal electoral districts and annual parliaments. The masses took up the cry with enthusiasm and a wave of almost revolutionary fervour swept through the north and the midlands, reaching a climax in the summer of 1839 with rumours that the miners, foundry workers and handloom weavers were collecting arms. Troops were concentrated in danger areas such as Newcastle[14] but after the failure of a big spontaneous strike in 1842 the movement declined.

The early 1840s, meanwhile, would have provided George Silvertop with much to consider for they marked the beginning of a great new era for the Catholic Church in England; Catholics still walked somewhat unsteadily on 'emancipated legs' but 'the greyness of uncertainty had disappeared and, in its place, the morning saw decision and a strange new courage that, in God's providence, was to press on to an achievement beyond all precedent.'[15] This mood of initiative and progress was further galvanized by the arrival in England of Nicholas Wiseman, the former Ushaw student now a bishop, and Dominic Barberi, the humble Italian Passionist chasing a vision of returning England to the 'One True Faith.' Wiseman had been appointed President of Oscott College, six miles from Birmingham; Barberi, with more than a little help from his friends Ambrose Phillips and George Spencer, had finally received permission from his superiors to open a mission in England and was staying at Oscott while he learned to speak English more fluently. Writing to his General in Rome, he said that, for the first time, he had been obliged to discard his Passionists' habit.

> I am dressed in secular clothing. If you only saw me you would smile. But I think that God recognises me well enough in these garments.[16]

The students at Oscott were accustomed to many strange visitors that Wiseman brought to the College, but Father Dominic was apparently one of the strangest they had ever seen. One of them, who later became Wiseman's Vicar-General at Westminster, left these impressions of Barberi at this time.

> He had an eagle eye; could blend sarcasm and irony in the most simple and apparently harmless observation; his grave demeanour when he spoke of Heaven made him seem compound of all that was humble and sublime in human nature. When he came to see us in recreation he amused us immensely. When we went to speak to him in confession, or to have our vocations decided, we came away in admiration; he possessed marvellous sway over us all, and could do what he liked with us.[17]

Also at Oscott at this time was George Spencer[18], the convert from an aristocratic Protestant family, later to be known as Father Ignatius of the Passionist Order, who had been ordained in Rome (1832) and was now spiritual director of the young men preparing for the priesthood. His biographer later wrote:

At Oscott as everywhere else, Spencer's influence radiated far beyond the particular bounds where his lot was cast. He visited the sick in the neighbourhood, preached special sermons in all directions, and, when at home, drew, by the magnetism of his personality and the interest of his career, a constant stream of non-Catholic visitors to the College. This was enlightening work of definite value, in days when a Catholic College was an even more mysterious place, and *terra incognito* to 'those outside the walls.'[19]

The third member of the trio – Spencer, Barberi and Ambrose Phillips – who, a decade previously, had spent hours in each others' company in Rome plotting the conversion of England, had since inherited a famous estate steeped in ancient Catholic tradition – Grace Dieu[20], in the heart of Charnwood Forest, in Leicestershire – and with Lord Shrewsbury's financial help[21], had established the first new monastery to be opened in England since the Reformation, [22] called Mount St. Bernard's Abbey, which he presented to the Cistercians of Garendon, of whom his ancestors, the de Lisles, had been benefactors.

And finally, making his own inimitable contribution to the Second Spring, there was John Henry Newman of the Oxford Movement.[23] Newman had been appointed Vicar of the

University Church of St. Mary's, Oxford, in the same year (1828) as Wiseman was made Rector of the English College in Rome and by the early 1840s was one of the most prominent clergymen in the Established Church, famous for his oratory in the pulpit. He was later to declare that 'from the end of 1841 I was on my death bed as regards my membership of the Anglican Church'[24] but his conversion was long and agonising. Eventually, however, it was the humble Father Dominic, four years after embarking on what most people regarded as his crazy venture to convert England, who had the brightest star in the firmament of Anglican Oxford kneeling at his feet. That was in 1845 and soon afterwards Newman was invited by Lord Shrewsbury to Alton, where there was a large party of prominent Catholics, including seven bishops and senior lay figures such as Lord and Lady Camoys, Lord and Lady Dormer, Sir Robert Throckmorton and George Silvertop's friend, Sir Edward Vavasour[25], all former members of the old Catholic Board and British Catholic Association, and also present were almost certainly Wiseman, Spencer and Ambrose Phillips. Possibly even Father Dominic Barberi.

We have no documentary evidence, of course, but it is not inconceivable that the Squire of Minsteracres was there too among those distinguished guests!

References and Notes:

[1] Peter Ackroyd, *London the Biography,* Chatto & Windus, 2000.

[2] *Ibid*, p. 305.

[3] Reginald Colby, *Mayfair A Town Within London,* Country Life Ltd., 1966, p. 158.

[4] In 1836 Upper Dean Street, Newcastle, the finest of Grainger's new streets, was renamed Grey Street, and two years later a monument, designed by Benjamin Green, was erected to commemorate his forty years devoted to parliamentary reform.

[5] S.Middlebrook, *Newcastle upon Tyne, Its Growth and Achievement,* Newcastle, 1950, p. 176 (hereafter, Middlebrook).

[6] Generally this status could be inherited from one's father, acquired by serving an apprenticeship in the parliamentary borough, or received as an honour from the borough's corporation, but practices differed from place to place.

[7] A pamphlet addressed to the reformers of Fawdon, before Grey's bill became law, said that the votes of the Newcastle freemen were bought at half a guinea each. In Newcastle, too, when there was no contest, it had been the custom to give a dinner to the burgesses after the election, or ten shillings a head to those who preferred money.

[8] Middlebrook, p. 177. The Miners' Association of Great Britain and Ireland was finally established in 1841.

[9] Bernard W. Kelly, *Historical Notes on English Catholic Missions*, Oxford, pp. 279-80.

[10] Silvertop, p. 23.

[11] Upon George Silvertop's death, the Rev. Rogerson emigrated to Paris.

[12] Lenders, p. 84.

[13] Thomas Swallow, *Autobiography and Reminiscences,* 1905, Newcastle City Library, L920 5971 (hereafter, Swallow).

[14] Middlebrook, p. 179.

[15] From *Emancipation Realized,* a Catholic Truth Society publication, p. 28.

[16] Urban Young, C.P., *Dominic Barberi in England,* p. 29.

[17] Ibid, p. 32.

[18] Spencer left Oscott in 1846 to join the Passionists. He contributed to the establishment of St. Joseph's Retreat, Highgate, and at the time of his death (1864) was Superior of the Retreat at Sutton, Lancashire.

[19] Urban Young, *Life of Father Ignatius Spencer,* London, 1933, p. 105.

[20] The name is derived from the ancient priory of Augustinian monks, founded in 1240 and confiscated in the dissolution of monasteries under Henry VIII.

[21] Lord Shrewsbury's generosity as a church builder was legendary; he even took to living a large part of the year abroad so that he could save money to spend on new churches, such as St. Chad's, Birmingham and St. Wilfrid's, Manchester among others.

[22] The Trappists from La Melieraye in Brittany, who had been living on the Weld estate at Lulworth, in Dorset, since 1794, returned to France in 1815.

[23] Established at Oxford in 1833 under the leadership of the Rev. John Keble, a scholarly and saintly clergyman, the Oxford Movement (also known as the Tractarian Movement) championed the revival of Catholic religion in the Church of England.

[24] John Henry Newman, *Apologia Pro Vita Sua.,* London, 1846. Part IV.

[25] Bence-Jones, p. 159.

Chapter Sixteen

Missing the final act

It is clear from George Silvertop's last surviving letters - to his friend John Lingard - that he never lost his taste for travel, his contacts in high places or his interest in current affairs. Queen Victoria was now on the throne and England was enjoying the fruits of the Railway Age, giving the Squire the opportunity to remind people that 'the railways did not make Tyneside; it was Tyneside that made them.'[1] (As early as 1811 – long before George Stephenson's first steam engine – a locomotive had been used to draw coal wagons at Wylam Colliery, near Stella[2]). Whether Silvertop ever travelled by rail[3] we have no way of telling, but four letters written in the month of May 1844 find him, now in his seventies, back in his favourite London hotel trying to get to grips with the intricacies of the Brindle Lodge affair,[4] a complicated legal battle involving the will of wealthy Squire William Heatley, of Brindle Lodge, Hogton, Lanchashire. Silvertop's particular interest in the case is unclear but the first of his letters to Lingard on the subject begins in jocular fashion:

> I sit down to say How Do – although I have really not a word of news to tell you, excepting that I hear that Lord Beaumont[5] is said to be about to introduce two clauses

in his Bill arising out of the questions relative to the Brindle Cause. I hope he will not do anything of the kind – but will you, _entre nous_, tell me in a few lines the merits of that question ... I have seen a Pamphlet, printed in Paris called 'The Brindle Case' but I have so little confidence in it that I am emboldened to ask you for a short true statement.[6]

A week later Silvertop wrote again to his friend, this time asking for 'an account of the money transactions of Heatley and his family, with an account of what sum he left to the Church and whether it was money he had made and whether the person to whom he left it was his benefactor.'[7] A third letter was despatched four days later declaring himself to be 'a most troublesome correspondent' but this time asking Lingard where he could 'purchase or borrow' an account of the 1841/42 trial between the Rev. Thomas Sherburne and Thomas Eastwood (the principals in the Brindle affair). He added: 'I hear it was elicited from Sherburne that he had heard Heatley's Confessions three days before his death.'[8] Finally, on 3 June 1844, Silvertop wrote to his friend to offer 'a thousand thanks to you for the trouble you have taken about the Sherburne Affair. I trust nothing will be done by Lord Beaumont about it, but being now master of my brief, I will talk to him.'[9]

Clearly Silvertop's friendship with Lingard was more than a pen-friendship; in one letter to the Squire earlier that year, Lingard recalls 'sitting with you one day in the churchyard at Lancaster talking about our joint stock investment'[10] (in Lancaster Bank) while in another, which bears no date, he replies to an invitation to visit Minsteracres:

> I feel greatly obliged to you for your kind invitation and would most gladly avail myself of it, if circumstances would allow me. But with the exception of attending as a witness at the Blundell trial[11], I have made it a rule to stay at home for some years past. In fact I never drive out, even with a neighbour. Do not think, however, that I am the worse in health for my solitude. I am ten years younger than I was ten years ago.[12]

Later that year Silvertop was back home for the formal opening (21 August 1844) of St. Mary's Cathedral, Newcastle, which was attended (according to the press reports) by all the local Catholic 'families of position.' Most, like Silvertop, had contributed to the £10,514 cost of the project, which was the brainchild of Father James Worswick, one of the Squire's severest critics in days gone by, who had sadly died the previous year. Nine bishops attended the opening ceremony, including Bishop Riddell,

Vicar Apostolic of the Northern District, and after the service all retired to the old Assembly Rooms for lunch.

In January 1846 the Squire was back in London, this time for some unknown reason, staying at a hotel called The Alhambra.[13] It was the year that future-prime minister Benjamin Disraeli predicted the ruin of agriculture as a result of Free Trade in corn, but Squire Silvertop was clearly of a more optimistic opinion. He wrote to his farm steward, Hopper Swallow:

> Hopper – I have sent two bushels of Australian wheat, grown on Lord Plowett's[14] estate in Suffolk (where I was yesterday) by the steamer which sails this evening for Newcastle. I directed it to be forwarded to Riding Mill state, where I hope it will arrive on Tuesday or Wednesday night. You will sow it in favourable ground, where I think the result will be successful.[15]

It was in June of that same year that the papal throne became vacant with the death of Gregory XVI and the election of Cardinal Count Giovanni Maria Mastai-Ferretti, Bishop of Imola, who assumed the name Pius IX, was greeted in England with considerable excitement. Known to have liberal sympathies and to be likely to reverse Gregory's conservative, pro-Austrian policy, English Catholics saw in the new pope's election a fresh opportunity to press for the restoration of the heirachy and the vicars apostolic promptly despatched Dr. Wiseman and Dr. Sharples, the bishop-coadjutor of the Lancashire District, to Rome on a deputation to argue the case. In the meantime the great Catholic revival in England received an unexpected boost with the arrival of thousands of Irish fleeing the famine in their country caused by the failure of the potato crop in 1845.[16] This influx presented a great problem to the Catholic bishops who had neither the priests nor the churches to cope with the thousands of people, often destitute, who crossed the Irish Sea, bringing with them the dreaded infection of famine, the 'typhus fever'. Many priests were to die from this new plague, among them Bishop William Riddell, whose remains have only recently been rediscovered at St Mary's Cathedral, Newcastle. It was in the face of the challenge presented by the influx of Irish Catholics that the new religious missionary orders recently arrived in England came into their own. Dominic Barberi of the Passionists was so moved by the accounts of starvation in County Kerry that he sent from his own small community a subscription of four pounds that they had saved 'by denying themselves some things which our Holy Rule allows.'[17] The devoted work among the plague-ridden poor by fathers of the Institute of Charity and the Passionists did much to overcome the prejudice in which they were held by many of the old Catholics and when Father Aloysius Gentili[18], of the Institute of Charity, held a public 'mission' in Newcastle's one-year-old Cathedral in January 1846, it was attended by 1800 people and 250 Protestants were said to have been received into the Catholic Church. We have no way of telling whether Silvertop attended the mission but a year later he was at Minsteracres, preparing for a yet another visit to Paris. He wrote to Lingard on 21 August 1847:

The last post brought me your letter of the 10th inst., with an account of your severe illness[19], of which I was totally ignorant; & which I most sincerely hope is past & that this may find you daily gaining health & strength. I consider your present as most valuable, and for it I beg to express to you the gratitude of a most grateful heart. I shall, when framed, place it in my Gallery of Dearest Friends & among many of the greatest & best men of our age – and among others Pius the 7th. I leave this on Thursday night, dine with the Bishop of Durham on that day & on Friday I hope to be at Lartington, Barnard Castle. Pray direct a line to me at that place (which I leave on the following day for Paris) by return of post, telling me how you are going on & stating if I can do anything for you in Paris. I shall return at the end of

September & hope in person to find you in good health.

His visit to Paris, in fact, was curtailed by an event that was to have major implications on the future of Minsteracres, which he explained in his last surviving letter to Lingard (or indeed anyone else) written from Lartington Hall on notepaper bordered by the traditional black mark of mourning and dated 20 September 1847:

> It was my full intention to have been with you this day[20] but a most unexpected and a most lamentable event has occurred in this family which has obliged me to remain hither . I allude to the sudden death of my nephew George Witham.[21]

As George Silvertop remained unmarried, young George Witham was his natural heir. Witham, of course, did have a younger brother, Thomas, a priest, but being next in line he was set to inherit the family seat, Lartington Hall, and would therefore be automatically barred from any claim on the Minsteracres estate. It is obviously with this situation in mind that in his letter to Lingard, Silvertop added:

> The two eldest sons of Mrs Englefield, my late brother's oldest daughter, are here. The oldest comes of age next month. They have been both educated at the Collegis

Nobili at Rome, under the Jesuits. They are very fine young men & speak English tolerably well.

It is two years later, from the diary[22] of the youngest of the Witham children, Winifred, who was married to Gerard Salvin, that we get the first indication of George Silvertop's impending death. On 2 January 1849 she wrote: 'Thomas and Henry Englefield[23] went to Minsteracres, Uncle George very ill.' Her entry four days later reads: 'Uncle George's birthday & fear it will be the last he will see.' George Silvertop died in his bed at Minsteracres on 20 February 1849, barely a month after his seventy fourth birthday. He had outlived both his younger brothers – Charles, a colonel in the Spanish Army, who died in 1839 and Henry (1844) – and his benefactors Sir Henry Lawson (1834) and Henry Howard (1842). Only his closest associate, John Lingard remained, who in a letter to a friend, Mrs Thomas Lomax dated 23 February 1849, wrote: 'My great friend, of sixty five years standing, Mr. Silvertop, died on Monday night. R.I.P.'[24]

In his *Reminiscences*, written much later, Thomas Swallow describes how the Squire's body was enclosed in three coffins, the outer one made of oak grown on the Minsteracres estate and how on Sunday 25 February a service was held at Minsteracres attended by relatives and tenants. He gives a moving account of the sermon preached by Silvertop's resident chaplain, the Rev. John Rogerson:

> The funeral oration was so touching that the feelings of everyone present gave vent to tears. I venture to assert that they were genuine expressions of real sorrow for the loss we had sustained. Just to give a small portion of the beautiful language and pathos that the preacher used – he said that the deceased possessed within himself every endowment to render him of service to those around him; he was of sound judgment and sterling good sense, in mind inexhaustible, in resources of heart approachable was he at all times, ever most just, ever most generous. I see around me the silent evidence of your grateful approbation. God only knows the nature and extent of his manifold good works, and God in His goodness will repay him. He has left behind him no costly record of his name, no high monument to proclaim his aspirations, no ostentatious foundations or endowment to speak to men of his munificence, his deeds are register where angels only read them, but gratitude has erected within your hearts a lasting if humble monument that no time or spirit of decay can touch. Like the sun he diffused around him a light and a warmth that rested alike upon the lowly as

279

upon the great, fostering and cheering and drawing forth a smile of happiness from the very tear of suffering. Enduring be his memory and ever burning to us be the light of his bright example. (For the full sermon see Appendix 3).

Despite the fact that there was now a Catholic church at Stella, the Squire had expressed a wish in his will to be buried alongside his father, mother, grandfather and other members of the family, in the family vault at Ryton (situated beneath the chancel in the Anglican Holy Cross Church) and Swallow describes the mournful mile-long procession of carriages that wended its way from Minsteracres to Ryton, a distance of some miles.

I as a boy was trusted to ride in the cavalcade. On the road to Ryton we were joined by his Tyneside tenants. Thus ended the life of a truly good man.

Another year of course and George Silvertop would have had the satisfaction of witnessing the final act in the rehabilitation of the Catholic Church in England, i.e. the restoration of the hierarchy - 'a day of joy and exaltation of spirit, the crowning day of long hopes, and the opening day of bright prospects'[25] according to the newly appointed Archbishop of Westminster, Cardinal

Wiseman. It was, however, a moment also denied two other significant figures of the revival – Father Gentili, of the Institute of Charity, who died at the relatively young age of fifty the year before, and Father Dominic of the Passionists, who died a few months after Silvertop, aged fifty seven – both men literally worn out by their efforts to carry the Catholic faith into the streets of the new industrial cities. But then they, along with George Silvertop, were at least spared the violent outburst against 'Papal aggression' that ensued from a nation still overwhelmingly Protestant, the protests reaching a climax on Guy Fawkes Day 1850 when effigies of the Pope and Wiseman were burned in public places.[26]

These and subsequent events, of course, form no part of Silvertop's life story, but in conclusion one cannot ignore their relevance to the Minsteracres of today. It was Lingard who said after meeting Father Ignatius (George Spencer) that in coming to England the Passionists had 'acquired the *auri sacre fames*[27] of the country'[28], but even more compelling is the comment of George Silvertop's great-great-great nephew, Charles Arthur Silvertop (1917-1956) at a ceremony in December 1949 marking the sale of the house and part of the Minsteracres estate to the Passionists. He said he believed that his ancestors, unbeknown to them, had built Minsteracres 'in God's design, to house the religious family, henceforward to live there.'[29]

References and Notes:

[1] John Harold Clapham, *An Economic History of Modern Britain,* Cambridge, 1926-38, vol. ii, pp. 519-529.

[2] It is believed the earliest horse-drawn waggonway was near Blyth, opened in 1614.

[3] The world's first proper passenger railway operated by steam locomotives was the Stockton and Darlington, opened in 1825; the East Coast Main Line from London to Edinburgh via Newcastle was opened in stages between 1841 and 1850.

[4] After William Heatley's death in 1840, at the age of 76, his will revealed that Brindle Lodge had been left to his niece, a Mrs Katherine Eastwood, but that the bulk of his estate had been left to a life-long friend, the Rev. Thomas Sherburne. A year later Mrs Eastwood started legal proceedings on the grounds of undue clerical influence and after considerable litigation the Rev. Sherburne compromised by handing over £6,000 to Mrs Eastwood. However, Mrs Eastwood's husband was not satisfied and drew up a petition, signed by about a quarter of the Catholics on the Brindle Lodge estate, requesting the Bishop to prevent Confessors making the wills of penitents in their own favour. Nothing ever came of his suggestion.

[5] Lord Beaumont, the former Miles Stapleton of Carlton, Lancashire, who had been created a peer in 1840 by Queen Victoria, was at the time chairman of a Select Committee on the Burdens affecting Real Property that reported to the House of Lords in June 1846. No mention of the Brindle Case, or questions relating to it, appeared in the committee's Report. Four years later Beaumont quit the Catholic Church in protest at the restoration of the heirachy in England.

[6] Cambridge University Library, Add 9418/15/68.

[7] *Ibid*, Add 9418/15/69.

[8] *Ibid*, Add 9418/15/70.

[9] *Ibid,* Add 9418/15/71. See also Note 3.

[10] *Letters of the Rev. J. Lingard to George Silvertop*, No. 386, Ushaw College Library (hereafter, Lingard)

[11] The trial, which lasted nine years, involved the will of the eccentric Charles Blundell of Ince Blundell, in Lancashire. He left his valuable estate to Thomas Weld, who was not a relative, and the heirs of his two sisters unsuccessfully contested the will. Lingard gave evidence at the trial.

[12] Lingard, No. 377.

[13] The great majority of Silvertop's letters from London bore the address of the Clarendon Hotel, 158 Bond Street, yet an edition of *Boyles Court Guide*, published April, 1849, lists George Silvertop as residing at 19 Grosvenor Street. No other record has been found linking him with this address.

[14] Lord William Powlett (1776-1842) was the son of Henry Vane, second Earl of Darlington. He took the name Powlett after being created. Marquess of Cleveland in 1827 and later became Duke of Cleveland. His family seat was at Howick, Winchilsea, and he sat in the House of Commons as member for Winchilsea (1790-2) and County Durham (1812-14).

[15] Swallow, p. 5.

[16] Fothergill, p. 133.

References and Notes (contd.):

[17] Gwyn, p. 170.

[18] Father Gentili (1801-1848), like Father Dominic Barberi, had met Ambrose Phillips in Rome and it was Phillips who was responsible for his coming to England with others of the same order in 1835. Bishop Baines, Vicar Apostolic of the Western District claimed their services for his college at Prior Park, near Bath, but after a disagreement with the Bishop (1840) they left and established a missionary settlement at Grace Dieu, Ambrose Phillips' family seat. Father Gentili is also credited with having introduced the clerical 'dog collar' to England as the habit of his order incorporated the circular collar.

[19] Lingard's last years were dogged by an internal condition which caused him considerable pain. See *Lingard Remembered*, ed. by Peter Phillips, Catholic Record Society, 2004, p.1.

[20] Ibid, p.173. According to John Trappes-Lomax the privilege of staying overnight at Hornby was restricted to very close friends like George Silvertop and Mrs Thomas Lomax. Other visitors were not greeted with enthusiasm.

[21] George was the third of Henry's thirteen children and eldest surviving son. He was forty-two years old when he died and unmarried. His father having died three years earlier, George was succeeded as Squire of Lartington Hall by his younger brother, the Rev. (later Monsignor) Thomas Witham.

[22] Durham County Archives, D/Sa/F/419.

[23] Thomas, the priest, was Winifred's brother; Henry Englefield was her nephew, eldest son of her sister Catherine and eventual heir to George Silvertop.

[24] *The Letters of Dr John Lingard to Mrs Thomas Lomax (1835-51)* ed. by John Trappes-Lomax, Catholic Record Society, No. 77, 2000, p.144.

[25] From Wiseman's inaugural Pastoral Letter – see Bernard Ward's *Sequel to Catholic Emancipation* II, London, 1915, pp. 305-308.

[26] Wilfrid Ward, *Life and Times of Cardinal Newman,* London, 1897, pp. 551-552.

[27] Virgil (Publius Vergilius Maro) 70-19 BC, *Aeneid,* bk. 3, 1.56.

[28] H&B, p.301.

[29] From handwritten reports in the Monastery Journal of Events (the 'Plateau').

Appendix

(1)

The following is George Silvertop's obituary, published by the *Gateshead Observer* on 24 February 1849 and reproduced by the *Tablet* 10 March 1849:

We believe that in announcing the death of Mr Silvertop, we are declaring an event which will stir with sorrow, in different degrees, the hearts of thousands. Few persons, indeed, occupying the position of a country gentleman, have been more extensively known, or have left behind more cause to lament their departure from the world.

George Silvertop, Esq., died of disease of the heart, at his seat at Minsteracres, in the county of Northumberland, on the night of Tuesday, the 20th ult., in the seventy fifth year of his age. He was Deputy Lieutenant of his county, a Poor Law Guardian of the Union in which he lived, and a leading member of many public institutions.

Mr Silvertop was the eldest son of John and Catherine Silvertop, of Minsteracres, and was born at Benwell House, near Newcastle, on the 6th of January 1774-5. Like most Catholic gentlemen of that period, he received the early part of his education at the College of Douai. He completed his studies at the Catholic establishment of Old Hall Green, near London.[1]

Mr Silvertop succeeded to his paternal estate, and came into the scene of active life, at the outbreak of the war between Great Britain and revolutionary France. That war, whatever might be the policy of it, was at first highly popular with the British nation; various associations were spontaneously entered into for its support; and volunteer companies were formed throughout the country for military defence against the threatened aggression of

---

[1] There is no existing evidence to suggest George Silvertop ever went to Old Hall Green.

France. Into these measures for national protection Mr Silvertop entered with the ardour, which distinguished him at all periods of his life. He was appointed captain commandant of a local corps (the Bywell volunteers) and is said to have exhibited in that capacity considerable taste and talent for the military profession. Indeed, his efficiency in his new duties was so well admitted, that he had attached his corps to him so warmly by his spiritual demeanour and conciliatory habits, that before the dissolution of the voluntary associations, at the close of the war in 1814, his companions in the cause of national defence presented him with a sword of the value of one hundred guineas, as a testimony of their confidence and esteem.

At the peace of 1814, Mr Silvertop went abroad. He was in Italy at the time of King Murat's brief and disastrous campaign against Austria, and, together with several Englishmen of distinction, was for a time placed in a critical position between the hostile armies. In the same year, Mr Silvertop visited the island of Elba, and was admitted to a private interview with the Emperor Napoleon, then the imprisoned sovereign of the island. The views and opinions freely expressed to him at that conference, by the remarkable man who, at the beginning of this century, fixed the astonishment of the world, were full of deep and stirring interest. On his return to England, Mr Silvertop published an account of his interview with the Emperor[2], which was much sought after and read with avidity. Shortly afterwards, in consequence of his reputation as a man of high character, and ability, he was selected by Lord Liverpool's cabinet as the medium of private communication between Great Britain and the See of Rome, on matters affecting the conditions of British Roman Catholics. Although the negotiation was unproductive of satisfactory results, Mr Silvertop acquitted

---

[2] There is no existing evidence of this. Indeed, the fact that his friend Charles Butler some years later asked him for an account of the interview would suggest that he did NOT publish anything upon his return to England.

himself of his difficult and delicate trust with acknowledged talent and address.

In 1829, the Catholic Bill was passed. In the following year Mr Silvertop was appointed by the Crown, High Sheriff of the county of Northumberland, being the first Roman Catholic gentleman who had filled that ancient office in Great Britain since the time of William III. The office was invested, at that particular moment, with more than usual responsibility, on account of the agitation for the memorable Reform Bill by which the whole Kingdom was thrown into a dangerous convulsion. In this mighty struggle Mr Silvertop warmly sympathised with the hopes and exertions of the Liberal party. He was, indeed, both by the circumstances of his position, and by reflection, a Whig, in politics; and though he commonly asserted his opinions with that gentleness and moderation which were the amiable characteristics of his nature, he continued through life a sincere and enlightened advocate of national and constitutional liberty. Mr Silvertop's last public appearance in a political capacity was on the hustings of Darlington in 1847, to nominate Lord Harry Vane for the representation of South Durham.

It was a matter of surprise to many, and to some of the intimate friends of Mr Silvertop a subject of regret, that he did not avail himself of the opportunities which were open to him, after Catholic Emancipation, of entering Parliament, for which his tastes, his general information, and habits of business, gave him remarkable qualifications. It is known that the late Duke of Cleveland offered him a seat for one of the boroughs in his patronage before the enactment of the Reform Bill; and after that event, occasion was not wanting by which Mr Silvertop might have secured for himself an honourable place in the national councils. He, however, declined the temptation, and except that he exercised to the last the duties of a magistrate and Poor Law Guardian, and was the earnest and liberal promoter of every public institution of merit, he continued through life in a private station. But he made private station a post of usefulness and honour. His conduct was a model for those who occupy what is associated with some of the proudest recollections of Englishmen – the post of country gentleman. His habits of self-regulation (that most arduous of moral obligations), his scrupulous punctuality in all he undertook together with his diligence and activity, enabled him to carry on, apparently without effort, a variety of meritorious occupations and pursuits, and, at the same time, to leave no ordinary duty of his station not well performed. As you approach his residence, the well built and regulated school, the careful provision for public worship, the comfortable cottages and the attachment of their inmates, told of his constant solicitude for the welfare of his humble dependants. His sympathy for merit struggling with difficulty was well illustrated by the history of Mr Lough, the now celebrated sculptor. Mr Lough was a native of the obscure locality of Muggleswick, near Minsteracres. There Mr Silvertop found him, and was the first to notice and earnestly and liberally to foster the recognised genius of the friendless artist. To his own associates Mr Silvertop was endeared, not only by his individual worth, but by the thousand indefinite charities and nameless cordialities by which his friendship was ever accompanied. Those who saw Mr Silvertop only amid the gay amenities of London life, or even in the genial shadow of his own friendly and hospitable roof, might imagine that the pleasures of social intercourse were among the most attractive objects of his life. The fact was far otherwise. His life was something better than a mere chase for personal and frivolous enjoyments. He appreciated, indeed, the charm of polished society; but he valued both himself and others for solid qualities, not for the gloss upon their surface. He had nothing of the effeminate fastidiousness of the simple and the useful, too common with those of his station, by which imitate the vices, while they shrink from the corresponding virtues of feudality. On the contrary, he saw in the lowliest cottage a member, like himself, of the great social system, and he showed that humble man the most cordial respect whenever he performed the functions allotted to him with honesty and good faith.

Courteous, indeed, he was to every one, and kind, and gentle, and patient towards the poorest person who approached him; but he was, far more devotedly, upright, generous, just and true. He was firmly attached to his Church, by education and by conviction; but he was no anathematiser of the consciences nor scoffer of the faith of others. He was, indeed, more than tolerant – he was charitable in the noblest meaning of the term towards his fellow-creatures of every creed and condition. If the refinement in his manners, and the appreciated worth of his character, made him a welcome guest in the saloons of fashion or the halls of rank and power, he was found, too, in the abodes where are few visitants – in the house of mourning, and sickness, and want.

> To misery's darkest cabin known –
> His generous care was ever nigh,
> Where hopeless Anguish pour'ed his groan,
> And lonely Want retired to die.

We are noticing the departure from among us of this estimable man, to record the leading circumstances of his life, not to pronounce his eulogy. That will be spoken by the families whose union and dearest interests his friendly inter-position preserved – by the neighbours whose differences he reconciled – by the enemies to each other whose hands joined in lasting forgiveness and peace – and by the thousands works of mercy which have followed him to the world of light and love.

Appendix

(2)

From *Memoirs of the Silvertops of Minsteracres,* published in 1914 by the Rev. George Silvertop[3] - the letter said to have been written by George Silvertop to his friend Charles Butler in 1823, in which he describes his meeting with Napoleon on the island of Elba in 1814:

My Dear Sir

In consequence of your repeated requests I send you an account of the conversation I had with the Emperor Napoleon in an audience to which I had the honour to be admitted in the Island of Elba, 1814.

I was ordered to attend at the palace, formerly the Government house, at eleven in the morning. On entering the hall, I was met by two officers on guard, who showed me into the adjoining room, in which were four other officers, two French and two Poles. After waiting a minute or two, General Druot, through whose kindness I had obtained the promise of the honour of being introduced, came in, and said the Emperor could not receive me for a quarter of an hour, and then left me with the officers. I was struck with the great anxiety of these gentlemen for every kind of information respecting France and continental news; they appeared very ignorant of events which had occurred during the last three or four months.

General Druot returned and said the Emperor was ready to receive me. We went through another room, in which were several servants in liveries of green and gold. One of them opened a door into the adjoining room, and on a curtain being drawn (probably put there to prevent the cold) I saw His Imperial Majesty standing before the fire,

---

[3] The Rev. George Silvertop (1856-1890) was the second son of Henry Charles Englefield Silvertop (1826-1887), grand nephew and heir of George Silvertop of Minsteracres.

dressed in his usual regimentals. General Druot preceded me and presented me, and then bowing, retired. I felt myself at this moment in the presence of the greatest man in the world – I made, I believe, the lowest bow I ever made in my life. The Emperor said not a word, but in dead silence (no one being in the room) stared me sternly in the face, and then in a tone the most haughty, the sound of which I shall never forget, said, 'De quel pays venez-vous?' I replied, 'Sire d'Angleterre.' On which he replied, 'De quelle partie d'Angleterre?' My answer was 'Northumberland.' 'Un pays très montagneux, célèbre pour les brebis, Je crois, et pour les montagnes?' On my giving him an answer, he said, 'Je le crois.' He now came one or two steps nearer to me, and with a most pleasing smile and complete change of voice, said, 'On me dit, Monsieur, que vous venez dernièrement de Paris – que dit-on de moi?' On my stating that I heard his name constantly mentioned, 'Ah! mais que dit-on? Parle-t-on de mes compagnes – Avez vous été beaucoup dans les Cabinets littéraires? Avez vous fait des connoissances avec quelques-uns de mes officiers? Parle-t-on beaucoup de moi?' On my reply in the affirmative to these questions, 'Et vous avez été à la Cour probablement, que pense-t-on des Bourbons?' To this delicate question my reply was, that what I heard of the King was in his favour. He immediately said, 'Je n'en doute pas c'est un homme d'espirit. Mais le Duc de Berry a fait bien des sottises, et quant à son frere il est plutôt fait pour Moine qu'autre chose. Que dit-on du Duc d'Orleans, parle-t-on beaucoup de lui?' To which I replied that I had heard him universally well spoken of. The Emperor seemed surprised, and warmly said, 'Diable, mais a-t'il du talents?' I answered that he had served under General Dumouriez, had been at the battle of Jermappe, and that, during his misfortunes, I had heard he had given his mind to the study of mathematics. 'On m'a rarement parlé de lui.' He then asked me where I had been educated; on my reply in France, at the University of Douay, where I had the good fortune to form an acquaintance with one of his distinguished Generals, the Duke de Trevise. 'Ah! c'est un bon enfant, un brave homme, je l'aimois beaucoup. Je lui ai donné ma jeune garde dans la campagne de Russie. Mais comment, vous êtes donc Catholique?' On my reply that I was, 'Je le suis aussi,' he immediately said, 'Un Gentilhomme me quitte jamais la religion de ses Pères.' He here began to walk up and down the room, and entered at full length for above a quarter of an hour, on the policy of our country as contrasted with his own. I have no means of describing to you the eloquence of his conversation, which exceeded anything I had ever heard. He entered at full length on the subject of the Test and Corporation Acts, making only one mistake, calling the Test Act, la Loi du Texte. He could not understand the policy of a country not allowing its subjects to be educated at its universities, and keeping in perpetual punishment many millions of its people. 'For my part,' added he, 'I follow quite a different policy. I found soon after I was in power, that I was at the head of a country without an established religion: churches made into temples of reason. The great mass of the people were Catholic. I therefore determined to make a concordat with the Pope. We had far too many bishops before the Revolution, I therefore determined to curtail the number – my plan succeeded most perfectly, and no measure of my government ever gave more general satisfaction. I recalled all emigrant priests and I gave them cures – I established equally the Protestants, and gave them a church at Paris – and to the Jews I gave equal liberty with the rest – C'est ainsi que j'ai calmé les passions en etablissant partout la liberté du culte. Mais dans votre pays je connais fort bien qui est à la tête de ces Prêtres et de ces fanatiques, c'est Monsieur Addington, on l'appelle à présent Milord Sidmouth. Je le connais bien, croyez moi, c'est Un Pauvre. From this policy I received the greatest advantages. The Jews became attached to me, and in my last campaign in Poland, rendered me great services; and as for the Protestants, they were the best subjects I had. Mais le règne des Fanatiques est bientôt passé.' He then asked me if I had looked in to the state of education in France, to which I replied, I had, and that I was struck with an establishment at Lyons. 'Oh!' said he, 'ce sont les Frères Ignorantins. I only heard of them two or three years ago. I examined into their principles and found them excellent for elementary education. I gave them that house at Lyons, and had I continued in France would have established them everywhere. They and the Sœurs de la Charité are admirable institutions. Avez vous diné avec le Duc de Trevise quand vous étiez à Paris?' I replied, he was out of town, and that I had not seen him. 'Et Marmont, vous l'avez vu?' I said that I had seen him but that I did not know him. 'He was under the greatest obligation to me, but he turned traitor – if he had remained faithful, which I never doubted, I should not have been here. Parlent-on beaucoup de Talleyrand? C'est le plus grand Coquin du monde. The King of Wirtemberg and the King of Bavaria both remonstrated to me against him, et J'étais absolûment fatigué de lui.' He then asked me several questions about the Allied Armies, and if I had seen the Sovereigns when they were at Paris. On my replying in the negative; he entered on the characters, and spoke very well of the Emperor of Austria, as a good man, but without any pretensions to genius. Of the King of Prussia, he said he could compare him to nothing but a corporal, who was always talking of making uniforms and pantaloons; and of the Emperor of Russia, he said he was 'très fin et très faux'. Of our King he said, 'On me dit que votre Regent est un Prince dont les manières son très gracieuses.' I replied it was quite true, but that these were the least of his qualifications; that I had had the good fortune to be admitted to the private society of His Royal Highness, and that I could assure him, he was a man of extraordinary talents. He evidently did not like the observation, and immediately said, 'You probably intend to travel to Rome and to Naples. You will see Murat, c'est l'homme le plus chevaleresque sur le champ de bataille, que j'ai jamais vu, mais quoique cela très incapable des grandes combinaisons. A Rome vous verrez le Pape; je lui ai donnè un Palais à Fontainbleau et un fort bel etablissement de chevaux et de voitures; mais il n'a pas voulu en profiter –

C'est un Moine, que voulez vous, mais quoique cela, c'est un brave homme. The King of Spain is there likewise, but he is very weak. His son, Ferninand is better, 'C'est un homme qui a du caractère.' He then talked much of Italy, and seemed fully convinced of its capacity to be made a fine kingdom, and appeared particularly attached to Milan. He then turned to the Congress of Vienna, said, he suspected they were plotting against Naples, and even against him in his miserable island. To this I replied that I was perfectly ignorant, but that I had been informed by a person in a high situation in the French Government, that the money agreed to be paid to His Majesty would be discontinued. He said, it was very likely – already they had not performed their stipulations.

The conversation now turned on France, and the many improvements he had made in it, and during the whole of this, he was very animated, and concluded by stating of all the benefits he had conferred on France, he considered the 'Code Napoleon' by far the greatest. That it had been the subject of his study both day and night; that he had assembled the greatest lawyers from all parts of his empire to consult with him about it, and whether he died in the island, or whatever his fate, that Code would carry his name to posterity. He than contrasted the state of England with that of France, said, it was impossible not to admire the energy of us Englishmen, the love of liberty which existed among us, but with great emphasis stated, that in his opinion the Sun of our Glory was nearer setting than the generality of the world thought. He then observed, 'I have given such an impetus to Continental exertion, that the different nations will supply themselves with their wants; and then will come want of employ for your people; and of course general discontent. In France I should have produced sugar for general consumption; but what I think must keep you down is, your National Debt. Mais vouz avez fait des miracles – Your volunteers, your united exertions against me when I talked about invading England, struck me with admiration for your people. Mais on parle contre moi en Angleterre, pour ma conduite envers mes soldats en Egypt. And I am accused too, in France I hear, of want of courage.' I observed his countenance turned red, and with much warmth he said, 'Do you think I should have been at the head of the French army for one hour if such were true? Do you think from an officer, I should have become Emperor of France? Do you think in the last campaign, the most glorious of my life, my army reduced by fatigue and constant exertion, would have shown that devotion to my person which they invariably did? – No.' With great emphasis, he said, 'ils sont des Lâches même qui en parlent.'

From this he passed to his campaign in Russia and asked me if I had heard much about it. My reply was that I had heard it much talked of, and had seen many officers who had been in it; and that all reported his army when they passed the Rhine, as the finest that ever went from one country to attack another, 'C'est parfaitement vrai jamais la monde a vu le pareil'. He then said, at Smolensko, a Council of General Officers recommended him to establish his Winter Quarters there, and to make his general attack in Spring - 'je pensai autrement', and advanced and fought the battle of Maskwa, by far the most bloody of any I was engaged in. Victory having decided completely in my favour, I thought everything was obtained. Here again he became extremely animated, and described in most emphatic language the feelings of his soul on this most glorious occasion. Here it was I thought the world was nearly my own – here it was that I thought any object that I had in view was within my power – here it was on entering into the Capital of the Czars, that the great objects that I had formed in my mind, were about to be realized.

I must here observe to you, that the Emperor had repeatedly ordered me, to ask him any questions I wished to be informed upon, but that I had not availed myself of his permission but in two or three instances. On His Majesty's repeating the last sentence with great emphasis, I ventured to ask him, what were the great objects His Majesty had in view for the happiness of mankind. He stopped, we were walking up and down the room, and

294

said, 'Monsieur, c'étoit pour Vous rendre justes.' He then immediately proceeded with a most animated description of the scenes at Moscow during its conflagration – went to the window of the room and said, when I touched the glass of the window, something like this, it was so hot that I could not bear my finger upon it; my house was near a league from the town. He then returned to the subject of England, spoke of our Parliament and of Mr. Fox, and asked if I had heard Lord Ebrington speak in the Parliament, who he said had been introduced to him two days before. I said I had not. Upon which he replied, 'C'est un jemme homme fort aimable, et il a de l'espirit.' I stated that he was the nephew of Lord Grenville, at which he appeared surprised, and asked if he had left the island. My answer was that I believed he was about to sail. He then observed that he thought Lord Grenville, 'Votre premier homme d'Etat'; that he considered him a man of great mind and penetration. Looking out of the window, he observed the day was very fine, and said, 'You would like to amuse yourself in going over the island,' and then dismissed me.

Such, my Dear Sir, is a true and faithful account of the greatest part of the conversation I had the honor to have with the Emperor Napoleon, many particulars of which, on my return from the Continent some years ago, I communicated to you, and which, in compliance with your flattering and repeated requests, I now venture to print.

Allow me to remain, with great regard,

Yours, very sincerely

Appendix

(3)

The sermon preached by the Rev. John S. Rogerson in the chapel at Minsteracres, in the presence of relatives and tenants, on the evening of Sunday 25 February 1849 (George Silvertop's funeral took place the following day at Ryton):

HEBREWS ix. 27.
'It is appointed unto men once to die,
and after this the judgement.'

These are words of revelation, announcing to us a truth of universal experience, and of every-day familiarity. It *is* so appointed – it is *a law*, taking its origin in the beginning of time, pervading all things, subduing to itself every created power, admitting of no exception. '*All* things hast thou put into subjection beneath his feet.' From the first victim, claimed by Death at the gates of Paradise, to the sacrifice that here lies before us, we have but too certain, too cruel and evidence of his dominion. Without perversion of the words of the Apostle, we may make admission, and say, 'Yes, Death! Thou *hast* thy victories, thou hast thy sting': - thy victories attain to the uttermost parts of the earth (for so it is appointed) and thy sting pierces, as a scorpion's, to the innermost affections. But thy sway is of earth, and it has its bounds: and, contemplating these bounds, the Christian thus beholds thee rendered subservient to him, sees thee ministering to his highest hope and aspiration, for through the gates of Death we enter into life. The material framework of the body is dissolved, and the soul walks forth in her native majesty to claim the protection of Him, 'who is the Author alike of Life and of Death.' Nay more, this very framework itself that exultingly he crushed into dust, shall rise again in the newness of life, and 'this corruptible body shall put on incorruption, and this mortal

296

body immortality.' Where then, O Death, is thy victory, and where thy sting?

It is appointed unto men once to die (and observe well what follows) and after this, the judgement. 'We must all,' says the Apostle, 'appear before the judgement-seat of Christ.' No man knoweth whether he be worthy of love or hatred. 'I am not conscious to myself of anything,' adds St. Paul, 'yet am I not thereby justified, for it is God who judgeth me.'

This dread uncertainty it is, that gives a terror to the aspect of death. Disarmed himself of all power over us, yet he is stationed at the entrance of that long and darksome vista that conducts to the throne of the King of Terrors. Hence have the holiest of men shuddered at his call, and shrunk from his summons. 'I go,' said the holy Job, 'and return no more, to the land that is dark, and covered with the mist of death.' The soul of him so recently sojourning amongst us, has been called forth to penetrate this dense obscurity: the veil, suspended between us in mortality, and the mysteries of the worlds that is spiritual, has been raised to admit him, and alone has he stood in the bright presence of the God that made him. Alone has he stood before his judge, and 'with his own eyes has he beheld the Redeemer that liveth – face to face – now does he *know*, even as *he is known*.' God grant that mercy may prevail! God grant that the goodly deeds of a long life may plead for him, and not in vain!

Already has the sentence irrevocable been pronounced upon him, already has a just judge 'rendered to him, as to every man, according to his works.'

My friends, my Christian Brethren, I am not here to give undue praise to the dead, much less am I here to wrong the deceased of the merit of his many virtues. You yourselves are the judges of the justice of my words, for side by side have you journeyed through life with him, and you have seen how he has 'borne the heats and burdens of the day', and the toils of his long pilgrimage. You know what manner of a man he has been amongst us. But two Sundays ago you saw him, in his enfeebled state, occupying his

297

wonted place amongst you, and you heard that familiar voice once again commingling with yours, but in tones that were subdued. You heard and you saw him then for the last time. On public or on private occasions that place was never vacant. The earliness of the hour, the character of the weather, or the nature of his own engagements never stood as a wall against him and his God; but this duty he discharged with a regularity that must have impressed you, and a privacy that proclaimed of itself how single and sincere was his devotion. I record this as characteristic of the man, for he acted habitually *on principal*; 'rendering to his God the things that were God's, as to Ceasar (his neighbour) the things that were Caesar's.'

How solicitous was he ever for your spiritual as well as your temporal prosperity, reminding you, with a kindly solicitude, of the lasting wrong that you inflict upon your families, in denying them the influence of your guiding example, and the opportunities afforded them of a religious education. He had no sympathy with those who, in their practice as 'in their hearts, proclaim that *there is no God*'; who begrudge their maker the one day that 'He Himself hath chosen'; whose trust is, reposing in treasures that the rust or the moth may consume.

'Live', says the Apostle, 'temperately, justly, and godly, looking for the blessed hope, and the glorious appearing of the great God and our Saviour, Jesus Christ.' Live *temperately* by an upright perseverance in self-government; *justly* by integrity, honour, and all honesty towards your fellow-man; and *godly* in all that belongs to you Creator.

Need I illustrate this triple duty, by an appeal in detail to the past, in order to establish in your mind the claims of the deceased to this 'blessed hope.' Again I say, you know what manner of a man he has been amongst us. It suits rather, that we yield to our most grateful recollections, and come at once to contemplate that distinguishing feature of his character, that will ever remain to us the first association with his memory; I mean his active benevolence, his unwearied, universal charity. This is eminently *the* virtue of the Christian: 'by this shall all men

298

know that you are my disciples (said Jesus Christ) if you have love for one another.' Again charity it is, that is to form the foundation of our 'blessed hope', for 'charity covereth a multitude of sins.' 'Blessed therefore are the merciful for they shall obtain mercy.'

My dear friends and neighbours, I condole with you from my heart on the sever loss that you have sustained: I feel with you, that we have, each and all, in him surrendered up to death a friend of well-tried, assured worth, a wise counsellor, a light that never failed us. Not the poor alone, not they only whose afflictions are of the body, but the desolate of heart, the afflicted from within, will long lament over him in their orphanage, as for a parent that is dead to them. Personally he had acquaintance with each and all of you; he knew your every want, your individual merits and demerits, your capabilities and defects; he saw with admirable penetration who would repay, and who abuse his patronage, yet he was ever willing to renew the opportunities that youth in its waywardness had spurned, or a virtue less courageous he had yielded up. He possessed within himself every endowment to render him of service to those around him; of sound judgement and sterling good sense in mind; inexhaustible in resources of heart, approachable was he at all times, ever most just, ever most generous. And how did he dispose of these many talents – how did he acquit himself in the high position assigned unto him in the wisdom of Providence, for our welfare? I see around me the silent evidence of your grateful approbation. God only knows the nature and the extent of his manifold good works, and God in his goodness will repay him. He has left behind him no costly record of his name, no high monument to proclaim his aspirations, no ostentatious foundation or endowment to speak to men of his munificence. His deeds are registered where angels only read them; but gratitude has erected within your hearts a lasting, if humble, monument, that no time or spirit of decay can touch. Like the sun, he diffused around him a light and a warmth, that rested alike upon the lowly as upon the great, fostering and cheering and drawing forth a smile of happiness from the very tear of suffering. Enduring be his memory, and ever burning to us be the light of his bright example!

When the disciples arrived in the town of Joppe they found the inhabitants congregated together to bewail the untimely decease from amongst them of the good widow Tabitha. 'Behold', said they, 'how she ministered to us in our daily necessities; and who now is left to befriend us?' And they displayed the garments that she had made for them; and they besought the men of God to call her forth from the dead, that she might again bless the living. And, 'Peter, kneeling down, prayed, and turning to the body, he said, Tabitha arise! And at his bidding she sat up and lived.' Were it given unto us, my friends, in like manner to evoke from amongst the dead, the soul of *our* departed benefactor, how gladly, *for our own sakes*, should we grasp at this divine prerogative; but ours be the prayer, not that he may be returned to the captive's lot in Egypt, but that his may be the resurrection that conducts to the life that is eternal. For this accomplishment do you daily importune the Almighty Father in his behalf, mindful ever of the many benefits you have received at his hands, and restoring to him thus some remuneration for his charities. For 'it is a holy and wholesome thought, to pray for the dead, that they may be loosed from their sins.'

Think, therefore, kindly, and gratefully, and profitably of the dead: *kindly*, in justice to him as in charity; *gratefully*, because of the many claims that he has upon you; and *profitably*, in consideration for yourselves. Soon, my friends, shall we succeed to this the general inheritance of humanity, though seated now around this image of death in strength, and youth, and healthfulness, promising perhaps, to our souls a store of many years: for thus most certainly 'is it appointed unto all men once to die, and after that judgment.' And when the Son of Man shall assume to Himself the seat of His Majesty, and all nations, and tribes, and people shall be gathered together before Him to be judged, how shall He address Himself to them? Shall He call forth those of power upon Earth, the enobled of men, that He may render them precedency because of high achievements or endowments, the miracles of their faith, the martyrdom of their endurance, the countless deeds of heroism that they have accomplished in the flesh; shall these be arrayed in the first rank? 'If', says the Apostle,'I should have all *faith*, so that I could remove mountains; and have not *charity*, I am nothing. And if I should distribute *all* my goods to feed the poor; and if I should deliver up my body to be burnt, and have not charity, it profiteth me nothing.' You have God's own revelation on what is to take place. (Matt: xxv. 34) 'Then shall the king say to them that shall be on His right hand, Come, ye blessed of my Father, possess ye the kingdom prepared for you from the foundation of the world. (On what title do they receive possession. Hear Him !) For I was hungry, and you gave me to eat: I was thirsty, and you gave me to drink: I was a stranger, and you took me in: naked, and you covered me: sick, and you visited me: I was in prison, and you came to me.' Them shall the just answer Him, saying 'Lord, when did we see thee hungry, and fed thee: thirsty and gave thee drink: and when did we see thee a stranger, and took thee in: or naked, and covered thee: or when did we see thee sick or in prison, and came to thee? And the King answering, shall say to them, 'Amen, I say to you, as long as you did it to one of these my least brethren, you did it to me.'

The he shall say to them also that shall be on his left hand: 'Depart from me, ye cursed, into everlasting fire, which was prepared for the devil and his angels. For I was hungry, and you gave me not to eat: I was thirsty, and you gave me not to drink: I was a stranger, and you took me not in: naked, and you covered me not: sick, or in prison, and did not minister to thee.' Then shall He answer them saying, 'Amen, I say to you, as long as you did it not to one of these least, neither did you do it to Me.'

And these shall go into everlasting punishment – but the just into everlasting life.[4]

---

[4] Durham University Library, Pam L 942.82 SIL/RDG.

Index

305

Key to cover picture

The characters, from the left ...

Auld Judy (Judy Dowling) and next to her Jenny Balloo
(Jane Lindsey), in top hat Whin Bob (Robert Adams),
at back Jackey Coxon (John Coxon), front in
coolly hat Pussy Willy (William Stewart), behind
him Cull Billy (William Scott), in Scots cap
Lousey Donald (Donald McDonald), centre
facing left Bugle-nosed Jack (John Nicholson),
back, with hand raised Hangy (William Smith),
behind him Bold Archy (Archibald Henderson),
front, seated Blind Willy (William Purvis),
in hat Shoe-tie Anty (Anthony Deeney),
Captain Starkey (Benjamin Starkey),
far right Doodem Daddum (John Higgins),
and front left the dog Timour, who
belonged to the engraver, Armstrong.